Human Rights
and Wrongs

EVERY PAGE I READ TOOK ME TO THOUSANDS OF STORIES I'VE HEARD and at times felt I'd lived myself. Each page gave me pause, because there was so much tied together there, and so much rope that it could choke you, take your breath away, make you want to scream, and send you looking for matches to burn down the courts that were designed to defend slavery, colonialism, and the capitalist system.

Human Rights and Wrongs book should be required reading for law students and psychologists.

— Felix Kury, Program Director, Clínica Martín-Baró,
San Francisco State University, U.C. San Francisco

HUMAN RIGHTS AND WRONGS DEMONSTRATES HOW THE STRICTURES of "professionalism" can limit the effectiveness of psychological expression. Aron and her colleagues are liberating her profession by telling the story, under oath, in Federal Immigration Court.

In the fashion of Eduardo Galeano, the story can absolve the victim and leave the perpetrator self-condemned. This style can be troublesome for domesticated professionals since it identifies the state terror of their government. No American exceptionalism here. The self-condemned are not "a few bad apples," nor do they represent a "tragic mistake." The foreign policy is consistent and international. This study by Adrianne Aron ends with a true story and a metaphor. She remembers being lost in the Yosemite Valley. That memory represents the many people lost in our criminal justice system and ICE. What she does not say is the unspoken truth that she also represents a holy helicopter rescuing the dispossessed lost in the forest.

— Blase Bonpane, Ph.D., Director, Office of the Americas

COMBINING THE QUALITIES OF A PSYCHOLOGIST, A POLITICAL ACTIVIST, and a skilled writer, the author draws the reader close to individuals' experiences while informing the reader about recent histories of governmental violence. In other words, *Human Rights and Wrongs* teaches the reader both compassion and justice.

— Tom F. Driver, The Paul J. Tillich Professor of Theology and
Culture Emeritus, Union Theological Seminary

A CLEVER JOKER ONCE SAID, "I DREAM OF A WORLD WHERE CHICKENS can cross the road without having their motives questioned." I, as a mental health professional, dream of one where psychologists will understand why Ernesto Cruz drinks himself into a stupor, why Eva refuses to speak about what happened to her in Honduras, why Mrs. Malek is afraid to return to Afghanistan. In a collection of serious yet entertaining human interest stories, Adrianne Aron's *Human Rights and Wrongs* engages the general reader while inspiring psychologists to think outside the box.

— Shawn Corne, Ph.D., Clinical Psychologist, Albany, California

THROUGHOUT THE BOOK THE AUTHOR PROVIDES GEMS AND NUGGETS of hope highlighting the power of story. The ideas are powerful and challenge the reader to examine the resilience of the human spirit and our relationship to others as human beings.

— Hugo Kamya, Ph.D., Professor, Fulbright Scholar, Simmons College School of Social Work

PRIZE WINNER ◆ ESSAY COLLECTION

Human Rights and Wrongs

Reluctant Heroes Fight Tyranny

ADRIANNE ARON

WINNER OF THE 2017 SUNSHOT BOOK PRIZE

SUNSHOT PRESS

2017 SUNSHOT BOOK PRIZE™ FOR NONFICTION

Human Rights and Wrongs: Reluctant Heroes Fight Tyranny
© 2017 Adrianne Aron

Published 2018 by Sunshot Press, an imprint of *New Millennium Writings*.

EDITOR-IN-CHIEF
Alexis Williams Carr

ASSOCIATE PUBLISHER | COVER & BOOK DESIGN
Brent Carr

CONSULTING EDITOR EMERITUS
Don Williams

CONTRIBUTING EDITORS AND SUPPORT
Laura Still, Rebecca Moody, Linda Parsons, Chloe Hanson, Joseph Mooradian, and others

COVER ART
Eric Avery, www.docart.com
U.S.A. Dishonor and Disrespect (Haitian Interdiction, 1981 to 19___), *1990*
Collaborating Printer: Mark Attwood
Lithograph and linocut published by Tamarind Institute, University of New Mexico.

3   5   7   9   10   8   6   4   2

ISBN: 978-1-944977-21-4 (Paperback)
ISBN: 978-1-944977-34-4 (Hardback)
ISBN: 978-1-944977-18-4 (eBook)

www.sunshots.org
www.musepaper.org
www.newmillenniumwritings.org

SUNSHOT☉PRESS

musepaper.org

The name on the boat, 'One Respe,' was a Haitian solidarity greeting: 'Honor and respect.' The woman throwing her child into the sea represented a saying used by fleeing Haitians: 'Better to face the jaws of the sea than those of Duvalier.' The Immigration authorities are towing the boat off Miami Beach. Reagan instituted the practice of forcing Haitians back after some were washed ashore on Miami Beach. Alas, the refugee crisis is even worse now than when Ronald Reagan was president.

— DR. ERIC AVERY

Describing his lithograph, *U.S.A. Dishonor and Disrespect*, which graces this book's cover.

Eric Avery, M.D., is Emeritus Associate Professor at the Institute for the Medical Humanities at the University of Texas Medical Branch, Galveston, Texas. For many years he was Southern Region Refugee Coordinator for Amnesty International USA, before returning to medicine to address the AIDS epidemic. He lives on the Texas-Mexico border and works at the intersection of visual art and medicine.

INTRODUCTION

TRAGEDY, ARISTOTLE TELLS US, COMES ABOUT unexpectedly. Suddenly a good person plunges into misery, and the beholder, witness to so much suffering, is inspired with an awesome mix of fear and pity. A psychologist working in human rights knows much about that awesome mix. It is set before one by trembling hands, and it must be acknowledged, contemplated, sniffed and probed, so that no part of it is left unexamined. Torture. Beatings. Grotesque humiliations. Women dragged by the hair. Men sodomized by police. People sometimes want to know how we stand it. All that suffering...

If it were not for a potent ingredient that Aristotle neglected to add, this would indeed be a wretched way to spend one's time. But amid the poisonous pieces of every survivor's tale there shines a life-affirming element, appearing at times only as a glimmer, and at other times as a brilliant light that has the power to transform the dismal swamp of misery into a durable field of struggle. This element is called Hope. And when it's found within a person who has been treated as no human being should ever be treated, the psychologist discovers tremendous courage and determination, a fortitude that spurs them to fight for their rights and dare to imagine the possibility of a happy ending as survivors.

What the dramatist calls tragedy the psychologist calls trauma, which means *wound*. Like tragedy, *trauma* comes from the Greeks and can take many forms. A student dissident fleeing from murderous soldiers, a woman driven mad by torture, an orphan fending for himself on the streets of Port-au-Prince, a child traumatized in Arizona because both parents are in immigration detention...

The twelve stories in this collection tell of people I have known in my work and travels. Some are refugees I've helped in their effort to win political asylum, some are people I've tried to help in other ways — with therapeutic interventions or clinical reports that clarify their psychological status. Some stories I've included simply to share with others the enlightenment I gained from a particular individual or situation. Though I've changed names, places, and other identifying information to assure confidentiality, all the stories presented here are true. All the asylum petitions mentioned were granted, with the psychological evaluations contributing significantly to their success.

The collection devotes a lot of ink to stories of Salvadorans, and Central Americans generally, reflecting the immigration demographic at the end of the 20th century in the United States. Because I was based in California, I was close enough to document some of the effects of this greatest immigration wave in our country's history. After attending to many stories of hardship and survival, I then had the mixed fortune of experiencing a life-threatening trauma of my own, which I relate in the book's final chapter. Like the other people whose stories are told here, I would not have survived my ordeal had it not been for the energies and commitments of many caring people. It was a sort of unintended immersion experience for a person trying to fathom what psychologist Ignacio Martín-Baró called the "limit situation." As he knew from hovering at the brink of catastrophe during the civil war in El Salvador, this doesn't necessarily describe a boundary between being and nothingness; it can also define the line between being and being *more*.

I feel honored to have worked with the good people described in this book, people whose valor helped me through my personal trauma, and whose presence in their adopted country has enriched the communities where they settled. They have all contributed to the loot I collected as "the best paid psychologist in America." I dedicate this book to them, with profound respect and appreciation.

— Adrianne Aron, Ph.D.

THE BEST PAID PSYCHOLOGIST IN AMERICA

Packed between heavy covers, metal prongs choking it at the neck, its thickened middle crushed by rag-content, and its sides jabbed by clips holding flimsy tags, a body lies inert on a table somewhere in the United States. The venue isn't important: an immigration office, a criminal court, one of the warren of cubicles that wind through the American bureaucracy — this is only a *body of information,* after all; where it lies matters little.

A million words are tattooed all over that inert body, and at the foot of one of the trapped paper sheets is a signed form. What does it say? Written above the judge's signature is a decision that will make somebody's day or break somebody's heart.

Will the judge have taken the time to read the five or six pages I wrote for that file, or will my effort to humanize this paperized person have been in vain?

The file tells the story of a life, including the time and place where it began, and how it unfolded through the years with or without a caring family, a supportive or hostile school or no school at all; a work history or a history of looking for work and not finding it; a residential history that reveals border crossings into unfamiliar neighborhoods, cities, or even countries. Much can be learned by reading the numbers and words typed in the little boxes of a police report or a Homeland Security form, but too much is missing from the story. You may see a father's name and the word *deceased* next to it, but it will not say the boy was seven years old when he watched his father, a simple farmer, fall in a hail of soldiers' bullets. On another form, you'll see in bold print the number of a penal code violation, but you may have to hunt around for the IQ score that signifies mental retardation. In that thick body of information, when my own words add to the folder's heft, it is because an attorney wanted to ensure that when the body got inspected, the psyche — a Greek word meaning *soul* — wouldn't be overlooked.

Sometimes, and these are for me very good times, the psychological report has a big influence on the judge's decision.

Most psychologists who do forensic work trained for it. Not me. I was drafted into it by a tenacious lawyer who would not take No for an answer when I protested that I couldn't help her asylum-seeking client. She wanted me to examine the young man, to find something that would help the Immigration Judge believe his story. The last asylum client she'd represented, a twenty-three-year-old Salvadoran woman, had sat stiff in the witness chair and, without making a single grimace or shedding a single tear, told how government soldiers burned the village to the ground and raped the women and girls, even little girls; how they'd killed the animals and shot her father. The judge got angry: "If all that really happened, you wouldn't be reciting it like a laundry list." It had to be a fabrication, he said; and he denied her claim for political asylum. From reports published by the U.S. State Department, the judge had learned that Salvadoran citizens had nothing to fear from their government. It was the mid-1980s. The government of El Salvador was receiving billions of dollars in military aid from the United States. It was a *friendly* government.

The lawyer was convinced that this new client was telling the truth, but the young man talked in the same detached monotone, with the same calm facial expression, as the young woman who had been ordered deported to her treacherous homeland. Like her, he had trouble remembering names and dates. He kept confusing the date of his brother's murder with the date his sister was disappeared. He told the lawyer he felt like there was a short-circuit in his brain, because several times a day, and every night before falling asleep, he imagined people were violently grabbing him or members of his family, trying to kill them.

After his brother's assassination he was afraid he'd be targeted, so he hid out in the mountains, terrified of being discovered. Like everybody on the run with death squads at their heels, he didn't have documents to support his claim of what he'd been through. The only way he could win political asylum was if his attorney could prove that he was telling the truth about the persecution he'd suffered in El Salvador and his terror of returning there. Wouldn't I see him? "You speak Spanish, you know what's going on in Central America, you're a psychologist. You've even been to El Salvador. If you can't help him, who can?"

But how could I be of help? Psychologists don't have some magical power to determine if a person is telling the truth. Why make this poor guy tell his story to someone who can't be of help? Psychologists are not sworn to the Hippocratic Oath, but I felt a personal obligation to do no harm. Though I did not doubt that this man was afraid to return to his country, and earnestly hoped he would be given the safety that political asylum provides, I saw no point in needlessly putting him through the anguish of recounting these horrific events of his life.

The lawyer would not let it go. She kept insisting there was a chance a psychological evaluation could be helpful.

I resisted, refused, demurred, and finally capitulated: I reluctantly consented to see her client.

×××

Roberto Reyes had been a student leader at the University of El Salvador. As part of MERS, the national student association, he'd been involved in protests against the economic structures that kept 60% of the country's wealth in the hands of a mere 2% of the population, and forced millions to live in extreme poverty: hungry, without schools, healthcare, or a future. The Salvadoran military, in its defense of the status quo and zeal to wipe out dissent, went after young activists like his brother and his sister, his fellow members of MERS, and ultimately him. Narrowly escaping a roundup of his student group, Roberto spent two years in utter terror, in hiding, hunted like an animal. He finally made his way to the United States. To safety, or so he thought. Soon after crossing the border he was caught by the dreaded *Migra*, the Immigration Service. After three months in immigration detention, Roberto was bonded out and brought to Berkeley, California, where he was now living. Night and day, he was tormented by memories. He woke up from screaming nightmares to spend his waking hours fearful, withdrawn, and isolated, feeling life would never return to normal.

I was able to document the presence of Posttraumatic Stress Disorder, a condition that was seldom observed in those days except in soldiers who had been in combat. I wrote a report about Roberto's functioning that showed a direct correspondence between his story of what he'd experienced in El Salvador and his psychological symptoms. I aimed to help the judge understand Roberto Reyes as a living being whose blood is chilled by the need to stand before Authority, and whose mind churns as it tries to process the pieces of a ravaged biography.

Citing the report as compelling evidence that Roberto was telling the truth and deserved protection, the judge granted him political asylum. It saved his life!

I was hooked.

Short of running a suicide hotline, there are few jobs a psychologist can do that deliver such immediate and powerful gratification. Saving a life! I started a pro-bono agency to train other mental health workers in asylum work. I presented the Reyes case in a symposium of the

American Psychological Association. The press picked up the story and it was national news: the first time Immigration Court in the U.S. admitted psychological testimony in a Central American asylum case.

Posttraumatic Stress Disorder, PTSD, had been documented in a Central American refugee, and if that was the diagnosis, it meant the client's story was credible; the trauma had to have occurred for the clinical picture to look like that.

As we who do liberation psychology like to say: In our line of work you don't make a lot of money but you sure make a lot of friends. When human rights is the focus of your practice, most of your clients are people who have endured great trauma, and your kind words and human solidarity can serve as antidotes to the abuse visited upon them by others. They have heard the screeching explosions of artillery in the mountains and the creeping hush of death squads on the patio, the sizzle of hot grease spattered on their cheeks when a violent spouse slammed a frying pan in the kitchen, the *whirr* of the electric motor that ran the torture instrument at the army base. Paralyzed by fear, they have heard the words used to justify the pain they suffered: *indio, faggot, bitch, terrorist, subversive, jihadist...* They come from many places, speak many languages. Our job is to analyze their psychological condition so that someone in a position of power — usually a judge or an asylum officer — will pause for fifteen or twenty minutes to pull from the great body of information the five or six pages we have written, and read them with some care, so that this frightened person whose fate is in their hands will not be reduced to a bunch of Homeland Security documents or a rap sheet from a police file.

With political asylum and its promise of a safe environment, a refugee can feel secure enough to start rebuilding the life that was so brutally interrupted. Not everybody succeeds with that difficult project, and psychologists who evaluate survivors of human rights abuses seldom find out how the story ends. Did she recover from the trauma? Was he able to move on successfully with his life? Usually we are left to wonder. But in the summer of 2009, twenty-five years after Roberto Reyes's victory in Immigration Court, I got lucky. I ran into him.

I was in San Francisco, at a street demonstration protesting the forced ouster of President Zelaya in Honduras, and there was Roberto, marching with other members of CARECEN, the Central American Resource Center. I was elated. It was beautiful to see him at a demonstration. He was asserting his right to protest, to stand up against injustice and oppression, and express solidarity with people trying to defend democratic processes. He had knotted a thread that had been cut by the Salvadoran military years before. I wanted to give him a hug, but I held back. I remembered how he couldn't bear to have his name called, how it terrified him to be touched. "You look great!" I exclaimed. He dropped his backpack on the sidewalk and gave me a huge Latino *abrazo*, a bear hug. "I'm almost fifty years old!" he beamed. I noticed he was speaking English. "And my son's about to graduate from U.C. Berkeley!"

It was a cherished moment. I recalled that it was activist students at U.C. Berkeley who had rescued

Roberto from immigration detention. They had heard about the Salvadoran student leader languishing at the place the refugees called *El Corralón* — The Corral. They'd raised money to bond him out, and he'd arrived in town alone and traumatized, speaking no more than a few words of English. Immigration wanted to deport him, and the U.S. State Department was furnishing the Salvadoran military with names of all the deportees. Armed soldiers would have been at the airport in San Salvador, waiting for him.

Of the thousands of Salvadorans applying for political asylum in the United States in those days, 98% were being denied. A pushy lawyer made me see him, and my psychological report convinced the judge that asylum needed to be granted. And here he was, safely exercising the human right of free expression that had once almost cost him his life.

"*Hombre*, it's your fault that I spent all these years doing human rights work and never made any money," I teased. We fell into step together as the picket line turned the corner.

"But you know what?"

He smiled at me. "What?"

"Today," I said, smiling back at that happy man, "you made me the best paid psychologist in America."

THE SURVIVOR,
THE PSYCHOLOGIST,
AND THE STORY

Torture survivors telling their story to a doubting judge when seeking political asylum face a daunting challenge: not only do they risk being denied asylum (which may result in deportation and possible death), but they might be discredited and disparaged — accused of fabricating, lying, malingering — which can be so devastating psychologically as to constitute a new trauma on top of the extreme trauma of torture.

But the judge also faces a challenge. What if this so-called refugee from persecution is not a tragically wronged human being, but an opportunist gaming the system? Is this petitioner deserving of protection, or is the judge a fool to think so? If the petitioner comes from one of the USA client states, the judge is on the hot seat: sworn to uphold justice, but pressured to believe reports from Washington that describe all those client states as human-rights-respecting democracies. Behind the judge's bench stands a flag whose stars and stripes seem to spell out the word *deny*. Gavels in the neighboring courtrooms pound to the word 'Denied!' 'Deny!' is the cry of the government attorney. And the judge sweats, feeling the temperature rise on the hot seat, knowing it can get high enough to incinerate a judicial career.

But if there is an expert present, the judge can relax, because the expert also has a story to tell, and its cool content may contain evidence compelling enough to justify an unpopular decision. Certified with diplomas and a license, the expert speaks the same language as the judge, probably belongs to the same social class. The two of them may even send their kids to the same schools. With credentials both formal and informal, the expert is someone the judge can trust.

What credentials do refugees from oppression have? Often, their presentation of self and their sworn declarations are all they have to attest to their integrity, and on the stand their powerful stories may be reduced to incoherent fragments as they become too agitated and overwhelmed to speak up. Recounting horrific events in choked phrases amid a flood of tears or with no emotion at all, the petitioner for asylum may avoid eye contact, confuse names and dates, forget important facts; may contradict in speech what was stated in writing; may look to the judge like a dissembling, suspicious character. Since credibility is essential in the asylum hearing, this can present a serious problem.

Here the expert witness's story may save the day. A psychologist testifying for the asylum petitioner can explain that those shifty eyes and cognitive difficulties are classic symptoms of trauma, and far from impeaching the petitioner's credibility they actually support it, for had it not been for the persecution suffered, these symptoms would not be present. The explanation reframes the refugee's story so it can be perceived more favorably, more accurately. Expert psychological testimony can also address past acts that the judge might view as counter-intuitive or illogical. *Why did that woman keep going back to her husband if he was such an abusive brute? Why didn't the family go to the police when they received the death threat? Why didn't they leave the country right away? Why didn't the little girl tell anyone about the rape?*

Citing research on trauma, domestic violence, family dynamics, terror situations, and the like, a psychologist can provide plausible answers for questions like these, and, for the larger existential problems, other sources can be cited. Primo Levi's essay, "Beyond Judgment," comes to mind, with its discussion of the distortions that occur when people try to apply common sense reasoning to conditions of extreme oppression: "as if the hunger in Auschwitz were the same as that of someone who has skipped a meal." Fed by books, films, and myths that only approximate the reality, Levi says, the current imagination "slides fatally toward simplification and stereotype," and "is part of our difficulty or inability to perceive the experience of others."

The psychologist's narrative connects the individual's current functioning with the events that contributed to it, to help the judge perceive the experience of the Other. When that experience includes torture this is a tall order, because most of us do not *want* to perceive that experience, do not want to believe that those medieval barbarities are still present in today's world. Survivors themselves often say something that reinforces our tendency to deny atrocities, although that is not their intention. "I was only tortured a little," they will say, and then go on to tell how they lay bleeding and broken, and heard anguished screams coming from the next room. Their inability to help was itself a form of torture, underlining their own powerlessness in the face of extravagant abuse being visited on the victims next door. Thus a man who is stripped naked and hung by his arms from a ceiling bolt, and left there for three days listening to the sounds coming from the hell in the adjacent cell, reports that he was only tortured a little bit. The psychologist cannot gainsay that understatement; it's the person's phenomenological reality. But the psychological report will mention the searing pain in the petitioner's shoulder — a pain he never had before he was detained, and which gets worse whenever something reminds him of what they did to him at the police station. Indirectly, this corroborates the survivor's story by connecting the dots between state-sponsored violence and his current psychological state. Likewise, a psychologist can connect a woman's fear of men in uniform back to the time in her country when she was shoved into the backseat of a jeep; or a child's depression to the time the soldiers shot up his school. In all such cases, a plea for political asylum follows naturally, for domicile in a safe environment is the *sine qua non* of the person's psychological recovery.

When the survivor's story has been laid out and the arduous legal process results in a grant of political asylum, the petitioner feels vindicated: a court of law has certified that a gross injustice occurred. The judge feels secure because the petitioner's story has been validated by an expert, and political asylum is an appropriate legal remedy for persecution. As a psychologist, I feel proud. I have used my knowledge and credentials on behalf of human liberation, offsetting somewhat the disgrace brought to the profession by psychologists who work with military establishments to carry out torture and other egregious human rights abuses.

✳✳✳

But what if I get a story like the one brought to me by a person — let's call her Miriam Amaya — which involved a terrible and fully credible torture, but also included details that were simply unbelievable? For her, those details were the crux of the experience and had to be included in her story. Can a psychologist help refute the incredible parts of a victim's story without dishonoring the individual's experience? How to help the judge perceive the experience of the Other in a situation like this?

Miriam Amaya told of being strapped down, in excruciating pain, while men at a Salvadoran army post raped her over and over. I had an entire file of women's stories like that, collected by the University of Central America's Human Rights Office during the Salvadoran civil war. Ms. Amaya's description of the blindfold, the accusations, the assaults and terror she felt, bore a painful resemblance to accounts of many others. But as she described the four days that followed the gang rape, she recounted things I could not believe actually occurred. And if I couldn't believe them, surely the judge wouldn't. The lawyer feared that if she told that story to the judge, it would impugn her entire testimony and wreck her chance of being granted political asylum. But as a psychologist, I feared that if Miriam Amaya was not allowed to speak of those four days, she would feel crushed into the same powerlessness she experienced during torture. For her, the story of those four days represented the *raison d'être* of her entire life: her birth, her suffering, and her survival. Miriam felt she *had* to tell her own story as she had lived it.

Up to a point, Miriam Amaya's account matched the story I would tell if writing a clinical history of this fifty-three-year-old widow. Together we would agree that:

Like many people living in El Salvador during the 1980s, she used to cover her eyes when riding in the countryside, to avoid seeing the corpses on the side of the road. Unlike most of her fellow passengers on the bus, who gasped in alarm and fear when passing a corpse, she would sit quietly and pray for the souls of the dead. At home she kept her children close by, and except for going to church, stayed in most of the time because, as she put it, "On the streets, you die." Several of her neighbors had been taken away in the night, in trucks, and never seen again. She blamed her chronic insomnia on the barking dogs. She knew the dogs were aroused by soldiers making house raids, but as she lay awake praying, she only let herself think about the noise that was bothering her, never of the activity that was bothering the dogs. When the soldiers finally came for her, she was shocked by their arrival.

In this tapestry, two threads are about to separate to form two distinct patterns. One, designed by the psychologist, develops a story of fear mediated by religious observance. The centerpiece of *this* pattern is torture, an experience that becomes for virtually everyone who has endured it, the most powerful, unforgettable, and worst experience of their lives. The other side of the tapestry, Ms. Amaya's, does not center around the experience of torture. Woven with religious fervor, her pattern centers on the Virgin Mary, who carried a life-giving bouquet into Ms. Amaya's life. Images of torture emerge, but only as flowers in a sacred design.

In my story of Miriam Amaya's persecution, she responds to the pounding on the door that comes at nine in the evening. She tells the soldiers to wait while she changes from her nightgown. She quickly slips on a dress and opens the door, and the soldiers come in and start pushing her with their rifle butts, demanding to know where the arms are hidden. She protests. She knows nothing about arms. They push her to the ground and begin beating her. Her children start screaming. When they see their mother being blindfolded and taken away, her hands tied behind her back, their screams get louder. To this day, in her dreams, Ms. Amaya continues to hear her daughters screaming in terror.

For the next four days and nights she is held and interrogated in the basement of an army post, accused of hiding weapons for the guerrillas. She believes she was suspected of subversion because she was openly religious and attended Mass in the cathedral. The army had already murdered the Archbishop, calling him a communist. The interrogators didn't believe Ms. Amaya when she claimed to know nothing about arms. They questioned her, accused her, threatened her. They poked at her with their rifles, and then, while some kept their weapons pushing against her body, others physically assaulted and raped her. With a hood over her head, she could not tell how many men there were. But it went on for a long time and it was terrible. Of the five days of torture, including food and water deprivation, sensory deprivation, death threats, mock executions, threats to bring an official to cut off her arms and poke out her eyes, and whippings with pointed sticks, the worst part of the torture was the first night — the rape. Had it not been God's will to have her survive, she says, she is sure she would have died. Throughout the ordeal of the gang rape she never stopped praying, begging the Virgin Mary to intercede and keep her alive for her children's sake. When the sexual assault finally ended and she was still alive, she knew her prayers had been answered.

Ms. Amaya's unique pattern for the tapestry of her oppression begins on day two of her detention. Here she saw the proof that the Lord was determined to keep her alive. Her torturers began striking matches. They were going to set her on fire, she explains. But over and over the flames went out; their matches would not stay lit. The Virgin Mary had come into the room and blown out the matches. And when her torturers tried to shoot her on day three, their guns misfired. The Holy Virgin stopped the bullets. The officer they sent for to poke her eyes out and chop off her arms never showed up. The Virgin did not want her to be blinded and disfigured.

In my version of the story, intervening between an inner self threatened with annihilation and the harsh external world issuing that threat, religious imagery and sentiment created a shield for Ms. Amaya, to prevent complete destruction of a besieged ego. She did not develop the classic PTSD that often follows experiences of extreme abuse and that most likely would have led to a retreat into mental blocking and psychic numbing. Rather, she developed a psychological condition with a distinctively religious character, leading to a retreat into prayer and miracle. Her strong belief system allowed her to assimilate a series of events which, in the absence of such a system, would almost certainly have produced grave psychopathology.

Because her experiences were assimilated to the realm of miracle, the will of God, etc., they fit into a socially acceptable belief structure which, although mysterious and other-worldly, is not usually considered pathological. Were it not for the dispensations accorded to religious ideation, Ms. Amaya's interpretation of the guns misfiring would be considered indicative of a loss of touch with reality. In reality, the guns were not *supposed* to fire; the mock execution was meant to inspire horror. Yet Ms. Amaya's belief that the misfiring was an act of God allowed her to be inspired by God's omniscience rather than incapacitated by the soldiers' omnipotence. Essentially, she was invulnerable to certain aspects of the abuse committed against her, due to her psychological distance from the realities of this world.

This distancing, or immersion in the "other world realities," appears to have come about after the trauma of the rape, for during that most terrible of all the tortures, Ms. Amaya did not feel the protection of God. She was not transported away from that experience, nor was it made less horrible by any intervention from God. Unable to assimilate this experience into her religious belief structure, except in terms of having *survived* it, Ms. Amaya continues to feel the emotional pain of the experience. When she thinks about it, she cries. She goes out of her way to avoid recollections of it. It has permanently changed her feelings about her sexuality: she cannot imagine ever wanting to have sexual relations again. Unlike the other terrible things that happened to her, this one — having occurred prior to the flight into religiosity this traumatic experience brought about — has left a deep wound.

Just as religious ideation helped Ms. Amaya through the physical and mental anguish of torture, so has it helped her come to terms with the existential questions raised by such experiences. When asked what she would like to see happen to her torturers, she responded by saying that was something that would be taken care of by Jesus Christ. All those difficult questions: *Why? Why me? Why did I survive when so many others died? How will life ever return to normal again?* asked repeatedly by persons who have suffered traumatic abuse, are rather easy for Ms. Amaya to answer. Because everything can be understood in terms of God's will, nothing requires a personal or original response.

Following her release from the military jail, Ms. Amaya was watched, harassed, and persecuted. Soldiers passed her house nearly every night and pounded on the door with their guns to see if she was at home. At prescribed times, she had to report to them, to verify her whereabouts. After three years she finally had enough money to flee the country. She now feels more secure, is functioning better, sleeping better. Here, she says, "there are no barking dogs to keep one awake."

My story of Ms. Amaya's persecution — which helped her win asylum — detailed the six forms of torture she endured, and recounted her miracle-based versions of what happened, in a context of life-preserving psychological defenses. It said she needed a safe environment in order to develop additional skills for coping with her traumatic past. Using Salvadoran human rights reports and research on Chilean and Argentine torture survivors, I was able to demonstrate that the threats and assaults she experienced were consistent with those used in other Latin American countries.

Bearing in mind the temperature of the judge's chair, I thought it best not to mention that the techniques were consistent with what was taught at the U.S. School of the Americas, where the torturers were trained. A story has to tell the truth, but it doesn't have to tell *everything*.

THE DRUNKEN FOG
OF ERNESTO CRUZ

Somebody called the police. A latino male, possibly drunk, had wandered into a laundromat, picked up a two-year-old girl, and was heading for the street. The shocked mother of the child gasped and began babbling frantically in a language nobody understood. An old woman grabbed the man by the sleeve and yelled out to be heard over the din of the dryers: "Call 911!" The little girl, upset by the commotion, started howling. She was still crying when the San Francisco police arrived four minutes later to arrest Ernesto Cruz, a thirty-year-old Hispanic male, for drinking in public and lifting and carrying a child.

"Lifting and carrying a child?" The public defender must have heard the disbelief in my voice. He'd phoned to see if I could go to the county jail to evaluate his client. Evidently, when you don't know the child and don't have permission, it's against the law to pick up a child, and the question here was one of motive — whether this was step one in a bungled kidnapping, or the innocent mistake of guy who was drunk and didn't know what he was doing.

"Alcoholic?" I asked, thinking he probably had DUI records from here to Sunday, and a psychological evaluation would be superfluous, another professional opinion to add to a stack of police reports. If they charged him with kidnap, the lawyer was probably looking for a defense of diminished capacity: a criminal too drunk to be responsible for his behavior. Not my cup of tea. My specialty was human rights cases: torture survivors, victims of hate crimes, ordinary people oppressed by extraordinary circumstances. Not drunks. Or criminals. Everybody is entitled to a day in court and an adequate defense, but this was an evaluation any mental health worker could perform. Why me?

"It's a first offense," the lawyer said. "The Public Defender over in Oakland says you know a lot about Central America, and my client is Salvadoran."

Ah, I thought, *a little closer to my alley.* Still, I didn't like interviewing people in jail. I knew the drill: present your ID and letter of approval, surrender your personal possessions, take off your shoes and pass through the security arc, put on a Visitor badge and clutch an alarm gizmo while you follow a beefy guard to a tiny room where he tells you to sit down and wait till they bring the prisoner. You're in jail. You try to get comfortable on the molded plastic chair, and you look at the one-way mirror, wondering what the spook on the other side is thinking as he watches you. But at least you've got a contact visit. The lawyers aren't allowed contact; they have to talk to their clients through bulletproof glass, using a telephone. I have the privilege of touching the prisoner, shaking hands, detecting whether he's cold, or sweating, or shaky.

It's a bit awkward, of course, when his hands are chained to his ankles and he's limited in how much he can move. Sometimes the warden will allow a hobble long enough for cuffed hands to do the paper-and-pencil exercises I need for my work, and some prisoners get clever with contortions and are able to bend a knee and raise a leg to the height of the table, so they can write. The staff knew Mr. Cruz as a cooperative inmate. They brought him in without shackles.

"Well, I'm pleased to meet you," I say in Spanish, smiling at the lean brown-eyed man in the ill-fitting yellow jumpsuit. He smiles back, and I can tell he's happy to be talking with someone who speaks his language. Since coming to this country two years ago he's been trying to learn English, he says, but he's only picked up enough to get by.

"And what brought you to the United States?" I ask. I knew he was not escaping political repression like his countrymen who'd fled El Salvador during the 1980s and '90s. The peace accords that put a formal end to the war had been signed a dozen years before, and the FMLN, the revolutionary party, now had legitimacy in civil society. Maybe he was an adventurer, or an opportunist, or a member (or victim) of one of the notorious Salvadoran gangs that had formed in the barrios of Los Angeles and proliferated in El Salvador when the gangsters were deported back to their country. He probably was not one of the rich bourgeois businessmen who travel back and forth for the sweatshops of the multinational corporations; those guys would not need the services of a public defender. Nor was he a tourist on vacation; the civil war had come to an end but its root causes — structural injustice and huge disparities in wealth — had not. Salvadorans don't have enough money to fill their bellies, let alone take vacations. Who was he, then, and why was he picking up little girls in laundromats? "I needed to make money for my family," he said, in answer to my question about his motive for coming north. *We all need to make money for our families*, I thought, *but most of us don't wind up in jail.*

I decided to try another tack, to see if I could locate him in the context of his native land. During that terrible civil war that killed more than 100,000 people, there was scarcely a person in El Salvador who was not in some way exposed to the carnage. I asked Ernesto Cruz the question I'd been asking Salvadorans for fifteen years, as a way to bring them closer, slowly, to the traumatizing events that destroyed their mental health. Gently, in a tone of voice that said I really regretted to have to ask this, I said to this man in the yellow jumpsuit, "Tell me about the first time you saw a dead body by the side of the road."

Mr. Cruz gazed down at the tablet I was using to take notes. "I was eight years old," he said, speaking softly. "That's when the mutilated corpses started appearing in the countryside. My father was already dead, the army killed him the year before."

"I'm sorry to hear that," I said, nodding my understanding. He paused for a moment, his hands side by side on the table, wrists red from the chafing of the steel cuffs. When he saw I was willing to listen, he went on: "We were four kids, I was the oldest. My mother took us to her mother in San Vicente to be safer. By the time they signed the peace accords, I'd seen so many dead bodies I couldn't count them."

"And the worst experience?" I asked.

"The army, when I was nine," he said. "They had twenty-two men and boys lined up with their hands behind their backs, their thumbs tied together. Twenty-two men and boys, all crying, pleading to be let go. The soldiers took their machetes and struck every one of them on one side of the head."

His voice trailed off, and his hands rose to touch his face, near the scar on his right jaw. I don't think he was aware of having done that. Slowly, he continued:

"Then they took out their guns and came back and shot them. They shot them on the other side of their heads, and when they fell... when they fell to the ground, the soldiers put away their guns and pulled out the machetes again. They stepped over the bodies and cut off fingers and ears as souvenirs. There were no men left in the village to bury the victims. Women worked for four days digging graves."

"How terrible," I said. "How terrible. And you were just a child."

"Hiding behind a bush. I saw the whole thing. But it didn't affect me. For two months, it was like it never happened. I played, I did my chores in the fields, I watered the animals and helped my grandmother. And then, two months after, my mother had to take me to the clinic. They said I was *trastornado*, mentally disturbed."

From his description I could tell it was a delayed-onset Posttraumatic Stress Disorder.

"The doctors here at the jail say you still have PTSD,"
I remarked. He nodded an agreement, and I asked if he
thought there could be some connection between the
[...] charges that got him arrested.
[...] ifted up a little girl?"
[...] why you did that." I didn't add
[...] ible relationship between that
[...] done with the little girl. For the
[...] rge there was plenty to forge a
[...] PTSD are famous for drinking
[...] ted to hurt her."
"They say?"
"They say that, but I don't remember picking her up."
People with PTSD sometimes cannot recall details
surrounding the traumatic event they suffered, but
there's no diffuse memory loss. Mr. Cruz looked puzzled.
"I was drunk, I don't remember it."
I asked if he drank a lot. "Only that day," he said. "A lot
of beer. And I hadn't been eating. For almost a week,
nothing."
"You felt bad?"
"Very bad," he said, lowering his eyes with a look of
dismay. His chained hands dropped to his lap.
"Tell me what was going on," I said.
Now he explained that he didn't know why, but he'd
been having bad thoughts. He kept thinking about
bodies and gunshot blasts. He'd been trembling and
his heart was beating so hard he couldn't go to work.
His limbs ached, and he was feeling scared of everything. He felt so bad, he even thought of killing himself.

His birthday was coming in a few days, and always on his birthday he thought about his life, and what he'd been doing over the year, and what he'd be doing in the year to come. A great feeling of sadness had washed over him. He missed his family. When he left his country, he said, his wife was pregnant, he'd never seen his baby daughter. And only once had he been able to talk to his wife on the phone. There were no phones out where they lived. His wife couldn't write to him; she'd never gone to school and didn't know how to write. He'd never gone to school, either, but he'd learned; his mother had taught him. Far away in El Salvador his wife was living on their four-acre plot of land with the chickens they raised for market, and the beans and corn they raised for food. And with the baby daughter he'd never seen. "They're living with so little," he said. "I came here to work, to earn money so we could take good care of our child and send her to school when she's big enough."

Just then an iron jail door clanged nearby, and Mr. Cruz sprang upright in his chair. A deputy passed by in the hallway, his shaved white head visible through the little window in our cell door. *Exaggerated startle response,* I wrote in my tablet.

Cruz had been working as a roofer before he was arrested. Now there was no money to send home.

"Your lawyer tells me this is your first arrest," I remark, expecting him to tell me about the lousy food and the boring days spent alone or with people who don't speak Spanish. What I heard instead was something quite different.

"My first arrest," he said, "but not my first detention."

"El Salvador?"

"Sí."

When he was thirteen years old the soldiers had come around in a big open truck, lassoed him with a long rope, and tied him to the rails of the truck, along with the other boys in the area — the Salvadoran draft. Children who tried to run away were shot. At the army base they were beaten into submission. Ernesto was held for five days of beatings, and then released because he was underage. Two more times they recruited him by force, and each time they let him go after a few days because he was too young. In his second and third detentions he wasn't beaten, but he was so frightened he couldn't eat or sleep. Screams of prisoners being tortured on the other side of the yard tormented him night and day. The mere sight of a military uniform would set him to trembling and shoot hot pains through his arms and legs. For him, traumatized at age nine, the days of detention were almost unbearable.

For three hours I sat in the little concrete cell with Ernesto Cruz and learned about his life of grinding poverty and chronic PTSD, a life that for more than twenty years had been disturbed by intrusive images of bloody corpses and sounds of screaming men, yet contained no history of aggressive or violent behavior. The projective psychological tests I administered corroborated his narrative account: no antisocial impulses. Despite the many posttraumatic symptoms that kept him in a constant state of arousal — mind re-running scenes of past atrocities and body aching and trembling with fear — he had maintained his loving feelings and preserved his human values. He hadn't succumbed to the militarization of the mind that leads children in war-torn societies to see violence as the only way for people to resolve their differences.

Ernesto Cruz had married, fathered a child, and had risked a treacherous trip on foot through the Sonora desert to get work in California, nailing plywood on other people's rooftops so he could keep a roof over his young family. For two years, kneeling on sponge kneepads and hammering with an aching arm, he put in ten-hour days without complaining, then watched TV in the two room apartment he shared with a couple from Mexico. Then one day, very near his thirtieth birthday but very far from the family on which he'd staked his bets for a normal future, he was so depressed and lonely, and so tired and beset by intrusive, uncontrollable images of the hell he'd lived through in Central America, he couldn't eat, couldn't work, wasn't sure if he could go on. He bought a couple of six-packs and started drinking, and drank himself into a stupor.

He had never seen his little daughter, hadn't been there when she was born or took her first steps. He'd never seen her smile or held her in his arms. Only in his imagination did he know the feel of her hair, the sound of her voice. In a drunken fog he stumbled down a San Francisco street, swilling beer from a Tecate can in a paper bag, oblivious to his surroundings. And through the window of a laundromat he saw a little girl...

THE RIGHT TO
DRY PANTS

THE PRO-BONO LAWYER WANTED ME TO SEE LOUIS Antoine, a client he was "honored to be representing." Mr. Antoine was charged with a felony and was in danger of losing his political asylum.

"He's scared to death of being deported to Haiti," the lawyer said. "I'm hoping to get a habeas corpus action to vacate the criminal charge. That'll stop the exclusion order, and he'll be able to stay in the United States."

Habeas Corpus? Habeas... Oh, right... high school civics: Magna Carta, 1215, the right to know why the king locked you in a dungeon. It was the ancient protection against government abuse, enshrined in the U.S. Constitution and revered for centuries until George W. Bush's Military Commissions Act of 2006 struck it down and President Obama's National Defense Authorization Act finished it off in 2012 by granting the state the power to put you, me, anybody, in the dungeon and throw away the key. At the time of Louis Antoine's immigration troubles, in 2005, it was still possible to secure and enforce a writ of habeas corpus. But what could that have to do with me? I worked in human rights psychology, not legal theory.

A street brawl, the lawyer explained, assault with a deadly weapon. If Louis had understood what he was pleading to, he'd have pled differently.

"He didn't have a lawyer?"

"There was a court-appointed lawyer, but he didn't speak Kreyol. And the trial took place in English, but Louis doesn't speak English. The court did provide translation — into French, another language he doesn't understand!"

"And the reason for the psychologist?"

"The court's gonna want to know why he didn't ask for a Kreyol translator."

"And the reason he didn't?"

The attorney sounded a little apologetic: "He says he didn't understand he could."

"And you think the court won't believe him?"

"They might believe him or they might not, but they'll believe you if you say there's a psychological explanation for it."

"And you suspect it's due to…what?" Number one on my guess list was intellectual dullness. A bright person sees a mistake and right away tries to correct it.

The lawyer had a different theory: he thought it was trauma-related. Then I realized: of course, Haiti. A *coup* had overthrown the democratic government and thousands of people who'd supported Aristide, the elected president, were jailed, tortured, raped, murdered…it was a bloodbath. Thousands had fled the island to escape the repression. Now it figured: the man already had

political asylum. He must have been associated with
Famni Lavalas, the party of the ousted president; they
were all being persecuted. "Have Mr. Antoine's interpreter call me," I told the lawyer. "I'll be glad to see him."

✗✗✗

Louis Antoine was built like a wasp. His tiny waist fluted
up to a narrow ribcage, and downward to long, slender
legs. His black hair was cut short, and his bright eyes
and bright smile dispelled any doubts I'd had about
his smarts. Even before he spoke he gave off an aura
of sharp intelligence, and once he began talking his
facility with language came across despite the static
produced by translation. He looked younger than his
twenty-five years, and nicer than what I expected from
a street fighter.

"Can you tell me about the altercation that led to your
arrest?" I asked him this after a little chitchat about confidentiality and privacy rights. I was trying to size him
up, get past his friendly demeanor. Despite the safety
of having an interpreter present, I needed to feel sure
I wasn't dealing with a dangerous, violent guy about to
pull something.

He was assaulted, he said, by a drunk who'd staggered
out of a bar right into his path.

The guy might have been a little crazy, too. He was
yelling something about niggers, and took a swing at Mr.
Antoine, punching him in the shoulder. When he pulled
out a knife, Mr. Antoine, who was unarmed, picked up a
piece of glass from the gutter and cut him in the face, and

right then a police car with swirling blue lights turned
the corner and cops jumped out. They didn't arrest the
drunk, but they put Mr. Antoine in their patrol car, and
he was so scared he peed in his pants.

"You'd had other encounters with the police?"

"Many encounters! Many! They're always bothering
me on the street, want to know where I'm going, what
I'm doing. It's called 'Walking while black.' I produce an
ID, and then they leave me alone. This time they charged
at me and threw me to the ground. One put his leg on
my neck, the other pushed down on my back with his
boot, and they cuffed me and made me get in their car.
I was scared to death."

"What did you think was going to happen to you?"

"I thought they were sending me back to Haiti."

"Let's talk about that," I said. A man in his twenties
who wets his pants in fear and is willing to admit it must
be holding in a big story.

Louis is the only member of his family who is still
alive. A brother died of tuberculosis; everyone else had
a violent death. His sister was raped and murdered by
the Haitian police. The *Tonton Macoute*, Jean-Claude
Duvalier's personal army, killed his mother and set fire
to his family's house. They beat his father so severely
that he died from the wounds. Louis lived as an orphan
on the cluttered streets of Cité Soliel, Port-au-Prince's
most impoverished neighborhood.

"Did you fear for your life because of what the *Tonton
Macoute* did to your family?" I assumed he'd been granted
political asylum because his family had resisted the
Duvalier dictatorship.

"I feared for my life because of what they did to me," he said solemnly.

"But the *Macoutes* were disbanded when Baby Doc's regime collapsed." That was in 1986, as I recalled. Louis would have been only six or seven years old.

"Not every collapse results in a death," he observed sagely. "These are the same thugs who are in power today, who made the coup against President Aristide."

"What did they want from you?" I asked.

He smiled: "Money."

"You were rich?" This was incredible. I'd been to Cité Soliel. Nobody who's rich stays in Cité Soliel. There's no running water, the houses are made of cardboard and sticks; the roofs are pieces of tin pushed together like jigsaw puzzles; the dirt floors ooze into mud puddles when it rains, and crowding is so tight that people sometimes have to sleep standing up.

"Not rich," he chuckled, "resourceful." His father had had part ownership in a small fishing boat. Twice, when he was a little boy and they were out fishing, *Macoutes* boarded the boat and demanded money for the right to fish those waters. The first time, they whipped Louis — fifty lashes; the second time they took him off the boat at gunpoint and held him for three weeks. They beat him, and warned that they'd shoot him if they caught him in their waters again. This was the punishment for refusing to submit to the extortion. His father had spoken out against the kleptocracy. The punishment for that was death.

After his father's death, Louis made his way in life as a wood carver, selling small pieces to tourists in

Port-au-Prince. When the Lavalas movement elected President Aristide and established social services, he participated actively in the youth radio project at the Aristide Foundation and led a peer counseling group for orphaned children. He wished he'd had time to learn how to read and write, he said, but he was too busy. Then the coup came, and overnight everything changed. The thugs raided the Aristide Foundation, shut down the radio. People like himself who were identified with Lavalas were rounded up as "bandits" and shot dead or forced into metal containers in the hot sun without water or shade. Thousands of people were killed, thousands more imprisoned. In power again, the captain who had flogged Louis on the boat spotted him on the street and arrested him.

Amid the stench and vermin of a filthy, desperately crowded jail cell, Louis spent the next five days being beaten, starved, humiliated, and threatened. There was no toilet, no running water. He cowered in the cell, terrified that at any minute the club-wielding guards would strike him a fatal blow. He had to sleep on the concrete floor along with lots of others. A prisoner had a coughing fit and died and lay there dead for two days because the guards wouldn't touch his diseased body. Prisoners had no right to food; a request for food was met with beatings. One man had his tongue slashed by a guard because he had begged for something to eat. Prisoners had no right to speak to a lawyer or to know why they were being detained. Louis did not think he would get out of there alive but then, just as abruptly as he was brought in, he was released, with no explanation.

He went immediately to the pier and arranged passage on a leaky boat to Miami.

"You were able to think straight, to make plans," I observed, a bit surprised.

"Except I kept forgetting things," he pointed out. He had his passage all set up, then had to go back to his friend's house. He'd forgotten his money.

After he was captured by U.S. authorities, he was sent to a refugee camp where he was kicked and handcuffed to a fence. Someone asked him in Kreyol if he was afraid to return to his country and he agreed heartily, yes, that's why he'd left. As he described how he applied for and won political asylum, I observed that his speech was clear and well-organized, that he displayed appropriate affect and maintained adequate eye contact with both me and the interpreter. Though the story was entirely believable, with an internal consistency and logical flow, he was not reporting the sleep disturbances and agitated fears I was used to hearing from traumatized people. He denied having nightmares, jumpiness, flashbacks, or serious physical complaints. He was able to plan for the future and think positive thoughts without being brought down by intrusive recollections of his parents' murders, the fire, the beatings, the abominable jail conditions, the mind-numbing depravities he'd witnessed and suffered during his short life. He hadn't lost the ability to love, to feel. He did admit to trembling during his detention in Florida, though, and also during his trial in the California criminal court: "I was really shaking, because both times I thought they were going to send me back." A screening for Posttraumatic Stress Disorder, which

I conducted just to make sure, proved negative. But if it wasn't trauma clouding his thoughts and preventing him from asking for an interpreter during the criminal hearing, what was it?

Many fancy psychological tests have been developed to help us learn people's innermost thoughts and assess their behaviors. The tests are so popular that they're often used as substitutes for a clinical interview rather than adjuncts to it, to the point that clinicians sometimes forget to investigate their clients' subjective experiences. I regarded the attractive young man who was leaning back on his chair and raising his white sneakers off the floor to give his long body a stretch.

"You know," I said, "it's very unusual for a person to go through the kinds of experiences you have had and to come out in one piece. I'm glad you're one of those resilient people who did not develop serious mental health problems. And you're obviously an intelligent man, a man who'd dealt with authorities before. When you didn't understand what was going on in the courtroom, why didn't you ask for help? What were you thinking?"

Mr. Antoine sighed and looked at his interpreter. Then he proceeded with a simplified version of *Haiti 101, Haiti for Beginners*. He was too polite to call it *Haiti for Idiots*, but that might have been what he was calling it secretly to himself.

"It's like this: I didn't know I had a right to understand. Where I come from you don't go to court, you go to jail. In jail if you ask for anything, they beat you. In the high places, the authorities speak to you in French and hand you documents written in French, and you don't understand French and you don't know how to read. But you don't ask for anything. When you're done, somebody tells you, 'It's okay, you can go now.' Here, when I went for my asylum hearing there was a Kreyol speaker who asked me all kinds of questions about what happened to me. Then it got finished and she told me, 'You can go now; you won.' I was relieved, enormously relieved. I had been shaking, I was so worried that they'd send me to Haiti. Then when the police put the handcuffs on me in San Francisco and took me to jail, I thought for sure they were going to beat me then send me to Haiti. I was terrified. At the jail somebody explained to me that they wouldn't beat me there, but I was still scared because I thought this was a preliminary to sending me home. Then I went to court for the assault charge and I sat and sat, and when it was over the lawyer told me in English, 'The case will be continued. For now, you can go.' What a relief I felt. What a relief! They weren't sending me back to Haiti."

"I see," I said. "You thought a bad outcome meant they'd send you back to Haiti, and you were afraid of a bad outcome, and you didn't know you had a right to a translator."

He nodded vigorously and agreed in English: *yes, yes.*

"But what did you think that person was doing sitting next to you and talking in French?"

He thought it was part of the proceedings! He didn't realize the French interpreter had been brought in for his benefit. *Of course!* If she had been there for his benefit, she would have been speaking to him in his language — wouldn't she? And why should he expect that *anything* would be done for his benefit? I recalled what Primo Levi had written about the things smart prisoners learned very quickly in Auschwitz: "to reply *Jawohl,* never to ask questions, always to pretend to understand." Mr. Antoine was a savvy prisoner.

With this remarkably resilient individual, the psychologist did not turn up signs of mental disorder caused by trauma, cognitive impairment, or serious mental health problems. But a common sense opinion could be offered that could help with the habeas corpus petition. It explained:

Mr. Antoine's paramount anxiety and preoccupation had to do with a fear of being returned to Haiti, where he felt certain he would die, if not quickly by violence, then more slowly through neglect as a political prisoner. His failure to speak up in court to request or demand Kreyol interpretation was not due to emotional inhibition, psychological trauma, or mental disorder. Rather, it is best explained by the fact that Mr. Antoine did not understand that he had a right to request a Kreyol interpreter. No such right exists in his homeland. Had he known he could ask for an interpreter, it seems very probable he would have utilized such a resource.

As the lawyer predicted, the judge was disposed to credit my report — to believe me, though he might not have believed Louis Antoine. Swayed by the psychological testimony, the judge vacated the criminal charge. It figured: the judge and I had the same color skin, belonged to the same social class, might have graduated from the same universities. Mr. Antoine was black, poor, orphaned, and illiterate. He was unaware — except as a passionate aspiration — of the legal rights that most

North Americans take for granted. His home address was in the poorest, most exploited country in the western hemisphere. The judges and decision-makers deciding his fate lived in the world's most powerful nation, and most were white and well-to-do. They had families, academic degrees. They might have been to the Caribbean on a cruise, might have met some of Mr. Antoine's countrymen, most likely people who vacation in Paris and fly to the States when they need medical attention — members of the tiny, educated, wealthy elite who speak French at home. Quite possibly, every authority Louis Antoine encountered in the U.S. justice system was under the impression that French was the language of the Haitian people.

During President Aristide's brief terms in office, reforms were introduced in the Haitian justice system, making it possible to prosecute human rights abusers and requiring that court proceedings be conducted in Kreyol, the *lingua franca* of the island nation. If Mr. Aristide hadn't been ousted by a *coup d'etat,* Mr. Antoine would not have feared for his life. He would not have had to steal away in a leaky boat to seek freedom and safety abroad. He could have stayed in Haiti, speaking the language of home, safely, with strong hopes — and dry pants.

CIVICS DISORDER, NOT OTHERWISE SPECIFIED

SOMETIMES, FOR SOME IMMIGRANTS, ADMISSION to the United States and even the grant of political asylum can be surprisingly easy. During the Cold War, a fear of persecution by almost any government in the Soviet sphere of influence could win you a welcome to the USA. For Afghans seeking political asylum because their country was invaded by the Soviet Union, asylum was a sure thing. Thus it was no surprise that Aisha Malek, who was seventy years old when she was referred to me for psychological evaluation, had been living for many years in the United States as an asylee. Now she was hoping to become a U.S. citizen, which required passing a test to show a certain level of English proficiency and an understanding of American government — criteria her family members were sure she could not meet. If a health professional certified that their assessment was correct, the government policy allowed for a waiver of the test. Her personal physician had already submitted a form certifying that in Afghanistan she'd suffered trauma that prevented her from learning English and civics. The form was rejected.

As required, the doctor had written his explanation in language understandable to a person without medical training, stating that Ms. Malek's Major Depression was causing severe impairment in her thinking, concentration, and short- and long-term memory. He explained that Ms. Malek "lived many years in war and violence, which resulted in her Posttraumatic Stress Disorder, and she suffers from flashbacks of her past trauma."

All that was correct, but the physician had erred in failing to connect Ms. Malek's disability to the taking of the test. While the connection might be obvious to a health professional, it needed to be spelled out for the government bureaucrats. Since the doctor could not be reached, I, as a person with some expertise in assessing psychological trauma, was asked to see Ms. Malek and elaborate on what the doctor had written. If I found a reason her psychological impairment would make it impossible for her to pass the test, I could recommend that she be excused, and with that recommendation the government could grant her citizenship without requiring her to take the test. No problem; it sounded like a cinch, just a matter of dotting the i's and crossing the t's. An hour or two of interview, plus time needed for translation, and I'd be able to supply the appropriate details on the form. And the best part was that if my findings did not concur with the doctor's, not much was at stake: Ms. Malek already had political asylum, she was not in danger of being sent back to the place where she'd been traumatized.

In Afghanistan, Ms. Malek had been living close to the Pakistan border, in a region of intense and prolonged fighting. Her husband often had to travel abroad on business, leaving her alone to protect their three children from the incessant bombing raids in the area. Eventually, Mr. Malek's foreign connections allowed the family to move temporarily to India, and once there, to secure visas to enter the United States. In 1989 they arrived in California as refugees from Soviet oppression. They settled into a three-bedroom apartment in a nice white stucco building, on the same street in suburban Fremont where Mr. Malek's brother owned a restaurant. A few months later, Mr. Malek died of a heart attack. He did not live to see the collapse of the Soviet Union or to celebrate the wedding of his only daughter to Ahmad R—, the bridegroom he had picked for her, a responsible businessman from a suitable Afghan family.

Some years after Mr. Malek's death, Ahmad became eligible to apply for United States citizenship. He was eager to apply and felt strongly that his wife and mother-in-law should do the same. The three of them, according to the law, would have to "learn and demonstrate knowledge of the English language…, as well as… knowledge and understanding of the fundamentals of the history, principles, and form of government of the United States." For him and his wife this would not be a problem. But it was clear to them that Ms. Malek would not be able to pass the test. Since her husband's death she had scarcely left the house. Her English repertoire consisted of "How are you?" and "Thank you very much." She was of course fluent in Farsi, but there were a lot of things she didn't, or wouldn't, or couldn't, understand, and Ahmad and his wife were sure she would never understand the American form of government. Ahmad found her annoying. But after all, she was a mother-in-law; lots of people have mother-in-law trouble. Ahmad's immigration lawyer had pointed out that, on the recommendation of a health professional, Ms. Malek could become a citizen without taking the test. Since she had been in treatment for seven years for Depression and Posttraumatic Stress Disorder, the son-in-law thought he had solved the problem when he had her doctor fill out the forms. When the forms were rejected, the lawyer phoned me to ask: "Since you're familiar with PTSD and immigration cases, could you write a letter that explains how this diagnosis renders Ms. Malek unable to learn and demonstrate a knowledge of English and U.S. civics?"

"I would, if a diagnosis like that could produce results like that," I said, "but I've known people who have learned all sorts of things, including the devilish English language, while suffering from PTSD. Even in spite of chronic sleep deprivation and tremendous concentration problems, there are people who carry on, go to school, learn a trade. Why do people think this woman can't pass the test?"

Lawyers don't like to tell you things that might prejudice you against their clients or put the clients in a bad light. And they try to be very careful not to make any judgments they believe belong to the domain of the psychologist. Instead of "he's really dumb" or "she's totally bizarre," they might mention that "he sometimes has trouble understanding things," or "she's rather unusual." In this particular case, the attorney had never actually met Ms. Malek; her son-in-law had brought in the papers. She didn't know why people said that her client couldn't learn. It's what Ahmad, the son-in-law, had told her when he came in.

✼✼✼

Ms. Malek was nicely dressed and wore a pleasant smile when her son-in-law ushered her into my office on a cold February morning. Ahmad was our interpreter, though usually it is not a good idea to have a family member in that role when personal matters are being discussed. But this time it turned into an asset to have someone who knew her well. He was able to confirm some of the information his mother-in-law supplied, and to add some information she could not: her address, for instance, and her phone number. She had lived in the same house for the past two and a half years, but did not know the street address. She had been in this country for eight years, but hadn't learned any English. "She tried," said the son-in-law, "but when she went to classes she didn't learn."

Something wasn't right…

I recalled that in the film *Testimony: The Maria Guardado Story*, Maria shares that she had enrolled in classes three times to learn English, but the effort invariably triggered the memory of her savage torture in El Salvador, where the procedures were directed by an American, speaking English. To the liberation psychologist, the question of historical context is always prominent in examining a deficit or impairment.

"I know you have lived through some very hard experiences," I said to Ms. Malek, as a way of acknowledging her hardship and letting her know it would be all right to talk about it. I watched her as she heard my words translated into Farsi. As much as I dislike using an interpreter in my work, I do value the opportunity it offers to watch people's body language. Ms. Malek's head bowed as she affirmed what I'd said.

"What would you say was the worst part?"

She didn't hesitate. "The cave. When the rockets were coming I had to put my children in a cave. For days at a time they couldn't go out. We had nothing to eat, it was terrifying."

"It's so good you were eventually able to get to a safe place," I said. "I'm glad for that. Do you sometimes dream about it, still?" It would be rare for a person diagnosed with PTSD not to dream about the traumatizing event.

She wrung her hands as she told me about dreams of her neighbors lying dead on the street because they couldn't get to shelter. She wasn't able to tell me how old her children were during those war days, only that two were in their teens and the third was younger. Her son-in-law let me know their ages.

I asked her to tell me about her life before the war. What was it like back then?

"Ah, like a dream," she said. "I went to school, and that was the best time of my life. But I can't remember anything. I've forgotten how to read and write. I've forgotten everything."

"Did you ever have a head injury?" On my questionnaire relating to her medical history, which her son-in-law had helped her fill out, she'd made no mention of any blow to the head, but she did acknowledge bouts of dizziness and a blood pressure problem that sometimes caused her to pass out.

No head injury, but in Afghanistan, she used to be able to shop, cook things. "Now, no more."

"When you shopped," I asked shrewdly, "did you go alone, or did someone else usually go with you?"

"My sister, my cousin, somebody always came."

I worked on a hunch: "You had trouble making change?"

"Yes, trouble," she acknowledged to her interpreter.

"When you add fifteen and fourteen, what do you get?"

She paused for a moment, thinking. "Thirty."

"And if you take twelve away from seventy-five, what do you have left?"

She paused again. "Fifty?"

"Do you know how many quarters there are in a dollar?"

"Fifty," she said confidently.

I wanted to be careful not to reach specious conclusions about Ms. Malek's mental powers. Back in the days of the great European immigration wave, people processed at New York's Ellis Island were given the state-of-the-art Stanford-Binet I.Q. test, which showed that 83% of the Jews, 80% of the Hungarians, and 79% of the Italians coming to America were feeble-minded! The test was written and administered in *English*.

Using a little ingenuity, I ask Ms. Malek if she knows in which direction the sun rises.

"I don't know," she admits. "Maybe north."

And where does it set? East. When I ask her what a goat is, she tells me, "Like a sheep, it's an animal." I've established that Ms. Malek knows some things. But not enough things.

Though she has been in the United States for nearly a decade, Ms. Malek has not picked up more than a few phrases in English. I later found out from her brother-in-law, the restaurant owner, that she attended school to the tenth grade, but she failed three grades along the way and then the teachers just passed her along. Neither trauma, depression, nor a blow to the head that knocked her unconscious explained what appeared to be a lower than average functioning in the intelligence department. I didn't know what explained it, but I was quite sure that's what I was looking at. If I could document it, she could be spared having to sit for an examination she would not understand and surely would not be able to pass.

I wondered why it was important to her to become a citizen. When I asked, Ms. Malek smiled at her son-in-law, who translated the question for her. "Because it's important to you," she said to him. That seemed to me a good enough reason. He was plainly good to her, and her way of contributing to the harmony of the family was to accommodate his wish for everyone to become citizens.

"And why do you suppose it's important to Ahmad?" I asked. "Because he wants us to be safe," she said.

She seemed to be thinking of the naturalization process as the final step of the asylum process. It occurred to me that if that's what it represented to her, then having the certificate proclaiming her a naturalized citizen might actually contribute to her recovery from the wounds of war, by assuring her that she was finally safe, no more hiding in caves. For the typical asylee, that assurance of safety begins when asylum is granted, but Ms. Malek was not typical. She was a unique case, and a psychological evaluation would have to proceed creatively to capture her unique deficits and document them.

Fortunately, there are non-verbal, culture-free tests that can assess a person's ability to reason logically. Raven's Coloured Progressive Matrices is such a test, useful when there is reason to suspect intellectual impairment or deficits. Like Piaget's tests of certain types of brain function, it has been used worldwide, in privileged societies as well as poor ones, with rural people as well as city dwellers. As I turned the pages of the booklet with the test patterns, I watched Ms. Malek puzzle through the challenges, doing fine when the solution was completely obvious, and resorting to "matching" instead of "solving" when it became necessary to use logic to get to the right answer. It was no surprise when I computed the scores afterwards to find that she had placed in the range of "intellectually defective." Her ability to problem-solve was far below that of other people her age; she was definitely at the low end of the intelligence spectrum.

"Can you tell me the Farsi word for this color?" I asked, showing her a little green triangle that I took from a box of colored tokens made of plastic. "Ah, *sabz*," I said, trying out the foreign word after the interpreter signed to me that she'd given the correct response. "Do you happen to know what this shape is called?" She shook her head. She did not know the names for a triangle, square, or circle, though she was able to name all the colors and gladly teach me how to say them. Only by color, however, was she able to sort the tokens; she couldn't discriminate them according to their shapes. And she was not able to replicate a simple design that I created using four of the tokens. I noticed that she did not grow frustrated when she wasn't able to succeed with a task; she worked at it good-naturedly, then shrugged when she had to give up. Just as she accepted the need for accompaniment to the store because she couldn't make change, so she accepted her limitations when answering questions about numbers, shapes, and the sunrise, and welcomed the help of others to compensate for her deficits. What she could not accept, because it is not acceptable, is missiles and bombs striking her neighbors dead in Afghanistan, and having to hide for days in a cave simply to survive. She had adjusted well to her natural disability, but very poorly to the disabilities inflicted on her by the catastrophe of war.

Here was a person who had been traumatized by violence and grown depressed as a result of loss — of neighbors and family members in Afghanistan, and later of her husband in the United States. Her physician's diagnoses of Posttraumatic Stress Disorder and Major Depression were well-founded. But did her doctor really think those diagnoses explained why she wouldn't be able to pass a civics test or learn English? "If the only tool you have is a hammer," psychologist Abraham Maslow once said, "the whole world looks like a nail."

Putting aside the medical certification form prepared by the physician, I used a fresh form and listed the two diagnoses offered by the health providers who were

caring for Ms. Malek. To these I added a third, as part
of my "Professional Certified Opinion" on Form N-648:
"Borderline Intellectual Functioning." With that, I was
able to link Ms. Malek's disability to her need for a
waiver of the tests, "in language easily understandable
to a person without medical training":

*Short-term memory impairment makes acquisition of
new information, such as vocabulary of a foreign language,
very difficult. For this kind of cognitive problem, no amount
of effort can compensate for the deficits. Owing to intrusive
and hyperarousal symptoms of PTSD, Ms.Malek has
difficulty attending to many things, even those things she has
mastered, and these symptoms exacerbate the problems she
has in learning and retaining the data of everyday life. She
cannot recall when she last saw a doctor, she cannot repeat
a series of three numbers a few moments after hearing the
numbers spoken.*

*Conceptual problems (as demonstrated by ability
to group objects by color but not by shape) signify an
inability to comprehend abstract principles, essential for
understanding, e.g., the division of powers, the right to
free assembly, or the difference between liberty and the
statue of liberty. Inability to reason by analogy or form
comparisons (as demonstrated by extremely low score on
Raven's Progressive Matrices) means that Ms.Malek may
understand that Candidate A won an election by receiving
more votes than Candidate B, but she will not know why,
in another election, Candidate X was declared the winner
over Candidate Y. The abstract concept of Majority Rule
will elude her, no matter how hard she works to try to
understand it.*

Problems in executive function (as indicated by extremely low level of intellectual acuity) make it impossible for Ms. Malek to reason adequately, or make plans or decisions, or to assimilate and analyze the facts and complexities of everyday life. She cannot make change for a purchase or remember her children's birthdays. She would not comprehend the meaning of a noun or adjective, or of an issue in foreign policy or a concept like federalism. She would be able to recognize the American flag, but would not be able to count the stars on it. Asked how many quarters there are in a dollar, she replied, "Fifty." Owing to her inability to grasp complex information, even in her own language, she would not be able to understand the principles of U.S. government or engage in the study of history.

Voila! It was not hard to explain, the physician just hadn't followed the directions closely. I sent in the form and assumed the case was closed, a piece of cake.

The government wasn't satisfied. In the proper box of the form, I stated that I had used seven different psychological tests to substantiate my opinion: a sorting test, Raven's Progressive Matrices, a Mental Status Examination... I named all the resources, but I hadn't *listed* them. The attorney e-mailed me to say she had pointed out the names of the tests, "but our logic is not their logic, and he insisted that you LIST the tests you administered: 1, 2, 3..."

Annoyed, I revised my report, listing the resources I used rather than merely naming them. Why was I being hassled on something this petty?

It was time now to do an evaluation of the mental functioning of the Immigration Service. For this I had

no standardized test, but I had some common sense,
and enough experience with bureaucracies to know that
when they start minding their Ps and Qs *ad absurdum*,
it usually means they want to look squeaky clean
because they've been embarrassed in public and are on
a campaign to clean up a tarnished image. This was my
personal theory, not something to stake one's reputation
on but good for raising one's spirits. What was the latest
news on the Immigration Service? What was in the
papers? On the Internet?

Once, I'd been asked to evaluate a juvenile offender, at
a time when the city budget was under discussion and
the size of the police department's backlog of unsolved
crimes was leaked to the press. The kid awaiting trial was
charged with felonious destruction of public property.
Was he only a moderate danger to the community? If
so, the court might place him in a group home rather
than send him to the Youth Authority. I didn't have the
file that told the particulars of the case, so I wasn't sure
what to expect: a bomb in a post office? arson at City
Hall? mayhem at the public library? What I found in the
dreary concrete cell at Juvenile Hall was a sullen boy who
had carved his girlfriend's initials on his desk at school.
That was his criminal act. Kids are easy targets when
exaggerated charges have to get filed because the Board
of Supervisors is hammering out the appropriations for
next year's budget.

The Immigration Service's nit-picking sent me to
the Internet to see if there was something the INS had
done lately to provoke an order to make every form
and every decision impeccably exact. This was when

the Immigration and Naturalization Service was still housed within the Department of Justice, as the INS. (It had not yet turned to ICE, as the Immigration and Customs Enforcement arm of the post-911 Department of Homeland Security.) All I had to do was type in "INS scandal" and up came the story of Emmanuel "Toto" Constant, whose house in Queens, New York was being picketed by angry citizens demanding his arrest and expulsion from the United States. Was this perhaps an embarrassment to the INS?

Emmanuel Constant, the founder of FRAPH, a Haitian organization modeled on the notorious *Tonton Macoute* of the Duvalier dictatorship, had fled to New York to escape trial on charges of torture, murder, rape, and crimes against humanity involving thousands of people. FRAPH's signature atrocity was the use of sexual violence against women, to punish them for having the wrong political opinions. Under the democratic administration of President Aristide, the Haitian government requested Constant's extradition so that he could be tried in a Haitian court. A U.S. immigration judge had issued a deportation order, but then withdrew it under pressure from the Clinton State Department, after Constant revealed on the TV program *60 Minutes* that he had been working for the CIA. U.S. authorities declared that he presented no threat to public safety. He was not deported to Haiti to stand trial.

Constant was tried and convicted *in absentia* in his country, and sentenced to life imprisonment. But he continued to live in comfort in Queens. Most Haitians trying to immigrate to the United States were summarily sent back, and here was a notorious murderer and torturer being protected by the U.S. government. People in New York were outraged and were protesting in the streets.

The Center for Constitutional Rights and the Center for Justice and Accountability would later win a federal suit against Constant on behalf of three survivors of FRAPH's campaign of violence against women. He would be convicted of torture, rape, attempted extrajudicial killing, and crimes against humanity, and ordered to pay the plaintiffs $19 million in damages. Still he continued to live in comfort in Queens; he didn't pay up. Later still, in 2008, the Center for Constitutional Rights finally nailed him in New York's Supreme Court in Brooklyn — on mortgage fraud! With a sentence of twelve to thirty-seven years for larceny and mortgage fraud, the former death squad leader was finally taken off the streets, but he never did have to suffer the penalty for the crimes he committed in Haiti.

Was there really a connection between the protest in New York against a mass murderer from Haiti, and the scrupulosities of the Immigration Service in the asylum case of a woman from Afghanistan? I like to think there was, and that my client and I got the trickle-down effect of the government's effort to look efficient. For the examiner in the Immigration Service, I dutifully supplied a list beginning with 1 at the top of the page and ending with 7 at the bottom.

The lawyer reported that when Ms. Malek went for her hearing, she was asked through an interpreter to raise her right hand. She raised her left. She didn't know her birthday. "She was clearly depressed and kind of fuzzy," the lawyer said. "It was pretty obvious to the examiner that what was stated in the Medical Certification was valid." She was excused from the test. So the examiner had done his job, the lawyer had done hers, and I had done mine. We could all be happy.

It was right that Ms. Malek was able to become an American citizen. She would never understand the workings of the government, but neither would I, really. How could a kid who defaced a school desk be charged with a felony? How could thousands of Haitians who had tried to flee the atrocities of the criminal gangs led by Toto Constant be turned back, while Constant himself was allowed to live free in New York? I'm willing to bet all fifty quarters of Ms. Malek's dollar that she would figure out right away there's something wrong with that picture.

THE UNSPEAKABLES

NAOMI AND NESTOR WERE THE ONLY CLIENTS I ever interviewed by candlelight. The power failure came too late for me to cancel their appointment, so I had no choice but to apologize and offer to see them on another day. They assured me it was no problem at all. Where they came from, houses were usually lit by a single bulb, and oftentimes it didn't glow.

So we sat in the semi-darkness and we talked about talking.

This couple had been sent to me because when they met with their asylum attorney, Naomi would not talk about what happened in Guatemala. "Ask Nestor," is all she would say, and then she broke down in tears. The judge needed to hear directly from Naomi — unless there was a reason she cannot speak. So the lawyer wanted an opinion about her reticence — whether it's part of a family dynamic, or a cultural pattern common in their indigenous community, or an effect of trauma, or something about her personality… I wondered if *La Llorona*, the mythical Mexican figure who never stops crying, was known in Guatemala. I also wondered if there might be something about the lawyer's office that frightened this woman. Refugees from state violence tend to get nervous when they see a uniformed security guard in an office building; a person from the *campo* in Central America might be riding an elevator for the first time. These scary things are enough to make a person clam up. They can make a home-office visit by candle-light feel comfortable and safe.

To prepare for our appointment I'd reviewed in my mind "communication cases" I'd seen in the past, and this brought me to José, a kid who'd been acting out in school, disturbing his bilingual class by talking incessantly — but only in Spanish. No one knew why, but he flatly refused to learn English. It seemed he was feeling angry with English, or maybe scared of it. He was ten years old, a recent immigrant from rural Mexico. It turned out that he believed that learning English would cancel out his Spanish, and he was afraid that when that happened, he'd never be able to talk to his grandparents again. *A solution!* We made a bilingual book about planting a garden. This convinced him that everything his grand-father raised on his plot of land in Mexico could grow in English, just the same as in Spanish. It was safe to learn English!

Maybe this Naomi had some misguided ideas and I could help straighten her out.

Or maybe silence had become such a habit that she couldn't break it. I recalled another Guatemalan woman, Margarita, who had trouble getting her lawyer to under-stand the habitual silence she and her husband practiced at home before he was disappeared. Her volunteer asylum attorney at the Lawyers' Committee for Civil Rights couldn't believe that she had never asked her husband where he was going when he stepped out at night. Margarita claimed never to have suspected that he was seeing another woman. In the lawyer's culture and that of the judge, infidelity would probably be the first thing to cross a woman's mind if her husband wasn't talking about his evening sojourns. But in conditions of state terrorism, where people are tortured for information, the less one knows about anyone's political activities, the safer everyone will be. The night Margarita's husband was abducted, she had noticed his nervousness when she kissed him goodbye. He was more nervous than usual, more agitated. Her perception was of a man who was fearful and in danger, not one who was anticipating a rendezvous with a lover.

It could be that Naomi was afraid of revealing information that could bring reprisals on people back in Guatemala. Habits formed under terrorism have a long shelf life.

I had to wonder, too, if Naomi might be holding back because to put words to a traumatic event can sometimes seem a betrayal of the truth, because no words can do justice to the magnitude of the atrocity. As I recalled from another past case, that had been the reason for Eva's silence about what happened to her in Honduras. Eva's mother had finally saved enough money in her job as a nanny to send for the daughter she'd left behind five years before. Eva, now fourteen, had been living with an aunt since she was nine years old, but never bonded with her or confided in her. In California she came to a mother she felt she scarcely knew, and did not confide in her either.

Mother and daughter needed to apply together for political asylum, but Eva refused to present a case to their immigration lawyer. She refused to speak at all in the lawyer's office, and when she was sent to a therapist, she wouldn't speak there either. After three futile sessions of total silence, the frustrated psychologist was getting rough around the edges. She asked if she could bring the girl to me, in case a change of venue might open a door. It was a lucky move, for reasons neither of us could have predicted.

"Eva," I said, "You have to verify who you are. For the political asylum application — for you and your mom to be safe — we have to know that you're you. You don't have to talk. If it's true that you're Eva Ramirez, I want you to hold up one finger. If it's not true, don't do it. Are you Eva Ramirez?"

Without looking up, sitting silently in the small office, staring at the floor, Eva held up a finger. Using that method, we went on to establish that she was fourteen, living in Oakland, and came from Honduras. Good. Were you in school in your country? (The aunt had reported that she was a very good student). She raised a finger. Did you have some bad experiences there? A fidgeting of hands, almost a raised finger, but not quite. "I think that might be a 'Yes, but I don't want to talk about it.' Is that right?" A finger.

Working on a hunch, I asked if she belonged to a group that shared the bad experiences, and she affirmed

that this was so. Not a sports group. Not a music group.
Not a math group or a drama group. A discussion group!
She made eye contact on this one!

So this mute girl was a talker, she liked to discuss
things. What kinds of things? No fingers were raised for
any of a dozen guesses. Just as I was about to quit, my
gaze happened to fall on a framed poster that hangs on
the wall of my office, a gift from Elizabeth Lira, a Chilean
psychologist who provided services to torture survivors
and families of the disappeared during the Pinochet
dictatorship. The poster depicts the *Universal Declaration
of Human Rights* promulgated in 16th-century Peru
by Guamán Poma de Ayala. The rights are illustrated
with his wonderful paintings of the Right to Liberty,
to Asylum, to Expression, to Education, the right to be
protected from torture, the right to equality under the
law and a decent wage, and twenty-three other visionary
concepts of social justice.

I led the stubbornly mute Eva to the colorful messages
that had been designed five hundred years ago for a
purpose not too different from this. Guamán Poma de
Ayala had wanted the king of Spain to listen; I wanted
a traumatized girl to talk. "Those students in your
group — would they agree with what you see up there?"
Eva studied the poster on the wall, reading the Spanish
text painted in the colorful squares, and examining the
illustrations. Feeling the solidarity, she was able to break
the silence.

Over the next few months with the therapist, she
revealed a horrific history of violations of many of
those rights a Quechuan writer spelled out half a

millennium ago. Her high school group had suffered severe abuse at the hands of the private army of one of Honduras's big landowners. She had escaped with her life, some of her friends had not been so fortunate.

Did Naomi also feel she couldn't trust anyone with her story? Could she talk about other things, ones that didn't have to do with the trauma? "What was it like," I asked her, "before you felt you had to leave the country? Did you used to laugh?"

"Ay," she said, "there wasn't much to laugh about. I stayed in most of the time, and Anita couldn't play outside because you never knew if it was safe; there could be a crossfire. That's what happened to my cousin Mario. My other cousin was targeted, but Mario was just passing by on his bicycle and he was hit by a bullet. Through the neck."

"What was his name, the one they targeted?"

"His name was… He was called…" Naomi began to weep. His name was locked behind an attic door in the mind, and she couldn't get to it. Her dead cousin was like a brother to her; they were raised together, they were almost the same age. How could she forget his name?

Gently, Nestor furnished Horacio's name, and looked at me with sad eyes. He said that the same thing happened to him a little while ago when he told me about his close friend who was killed in the attack on the meeting hall. "I started to tell you his name; my mind went blank. And just this morning I'd been talking about him." I told him it's a common problem among people who have been through terrible experiences, and that I'd try to help the judge understand it. "And how are we to understand Naomi's silences?" I asked.

What emerged was something similar to the Mexican kid with his magical thinking. Naomi wasn't afraid she'd lose her language by talking about the past; she's afraid it will keep the past alive and she'll never be able to forget it. We talked about that enough to see she was conflicted about it, because she also subscribed to the wise belief that holding things in can lead to sickness. It was in her power to speak about the past, if she willed it.

Avoiding the traumatic events per se, I asked about other things, like the decision to leave the country. I learned that they discussed it at length. Nestor thought it would be best for him to leave first, and for Naomi to follow. The idea of remaining behind without him filled her with terror, because being the partner of someone who'd fled made one a target for repression.

She'd already thought about the difficulties of the journey, how she'd be the main one responsible for the children's survival. She was willing to risk it. Anita was three, Norma a babe in arms, still nursing. Nestor insisted it was safer for her to stay behind, but the fear of remaining alone overwhelmed her. Twice already, soldiers had broken into the house, crashing through the front door with pointed guns. "Where's Nestor? Where are the weapons? Where's the ammunition?" The house had none of that, but the men ransacked it, throwing things on the floor and making Naomi lie on the floor in the spilled cornmeal, on broken dishes. The couple was at an impasse until they saw the note left next to the dead body of Naomi's cousin Horacio.

The killers said they would come back for the rest of the family. These were the most traumatic elements of her life story, and holding them in, she admitted, had not diminished the memories. She was helped to see that speaking of them for the asylum hearing was key to the family's future safety. She, who had struggled through the Sonora desert with two babies, certainly had the power to tell of the house invasions and the death of her cousin. I appealed to her strength, which she had demonstrated so admirably in the desert crossing, and as she felt more confidence in the interview, she became more willing to speak. Her voice was low, and her face was flat like a painting. Flickering in the candlelight it showed little expression, but I could see she was blinking back tears. Nestor, in his work clothes, fiddled with the hammer loops on his carpenter's pants, watching his wife, surprised to see her talking.

"When you think back," I asked Naomi, "what was the most frightening thing for you?" This is always an interesting question, because each of us has a unique hierarchy of horrors, and people's answers are often a surprise. This is why torturers are taught to figure out their victims' worst fear. It is why the Americans used dogs against the Muslims at Abu Ghraib, and why the prisoners in Orwell's *1984* lived in terror of Room 101, whose contents they only imagined, never saw. For Naomi, the worst memory of all was the house invasion. Theirs was not the only town under attack. It was a war of genocide, and hundreds of villages of indigenous people were destroyed. Arson and rape were rampant; there were regions in the highlands where there were no virgins; soldiers had raped every girl they found. They had not threatened to rape Naomi, but the invasion so traumatized her that she wasn't able to attend the funeral of the wife and three daughters of Ramón, Nestor's good friend, all of whom had been raped before they were shot to death.

Nestor said that Naomi is not the only person in the family who avoids talking. He, too, was a person who avoided talking, because back home speech was very dangerous. "If they catch you, they torture you and make you talk, and as soon as you give somebody's name, they go after him." He added that even here in California he used to keep his mouth shut, because you never knew who might be listening. He had to rethink the whole question of talking when his kids were getting ready to call the police on him. I could tell he was kidding, his mischievous grin gave him away. But what did he mean? He would explain, he said, and he proceeded to tell this story:

My daughters came to me like a union delegation going to the boss. Anita, the big one, is the talker. Norma stood next to her like a bodyguard. "Papi," the big one said with a frown on her face and her lips tight, "Why are you hitting Mommy?"

"Mi hija," I said to her, "I never hit your Mommy. Why do you say that?"

"We want you to stop hitting Mommy."

"But Anita, I've never touched your mommy. Never have I ever hit your mommy."

"Then why is she crying all the time?"

"Oh, mi hija," I said to her. "Come and sit with me."

I put the both of them on my lap, one on each knee, and I explained to them that their mommy was very sad because some bad things happened in Guatemala. Naturally, they wanted to know what the bad things were, and these are things you can't tell a child. I had to find a way to explain to them why their mommy cries, so I told them there were some bad people who went around hurting the ones they called indios.

It was a touchy thing to explain. I don't want my girls growing up thinking that Guatemala is a place full of bad people. I explained that there were some very rich people who wanted all the land and all the good things for themselves, and they got the army to go out and kill anybody who believed that the land and the food and the good things should be shared. The rich people wanted the land and the cornfields and the animals all for themselves; they didn't want to share.

"Mommy always says Norma and I should share," my Anita told me.

"And that's why she gets so sad," I told her, "because the army was hurting people who wanted to share. You understand?"

Done with his animated tale, Nestor said to me, "They understood my story. You understand?"

"I understand," I said. "You tell a good story." He went on to say that he is by nature a talker. Norma, he said, favors her mother, because she talks very little, while the older child, Anita, is more like him: she talks and questions a great deal.

When this family was fleeing from Guatemala and hiding from Mexican immigration authorities in the

desert, Anita was already past the age at which acceler-
ated development of complex sentences occurs. Norma,
an infant, had to be gagged so she wouldn't let out a cry
that would give away their location. They used to stuff
a diaper in her mouth when she started to cry.

It may be true that she takes after her mother, but
she may grow up with her own issues having to do with
speech — a reticence that might be a legacy not of her
genes, but of the gags in the Sonora desert.

Naomi agreed to practice telling her story to the
lawyer. On making this decision, she smiled. It was
the first time I saw her smile. She explained that a new
dilemma had arisen at home. Before, Anita was after her
daddy. Now Norma, the little one, was after her mom.
Norma wanted to know why her big sister gets to go to
school, but she, Norma, has to stay home. She had been
nagging her mother, and Naomi, confessing she was at
a loss for words, was amused. Still smiling, she imitated
her five-year-old daughter: "You said we're supposed to
share, Mommy."

THE TIGER AND
THE MONKEY

IMMIGRANTS WHO ENTER THE UNITED STATES
without permission often get painted by the media and
ambitious politicians as dangerous criminals — thieves
who have sneaked into the country the way a burglar
sneaks into your home, to take what is rightfully yours.
What is to be done with an invader who has forced his
way into your place to subjugate and harm you? How can
you protect yourself? What has to happen before you
can feel safe? Joe Arpaio, who served six terms as sheriff
of Maricopa County, Arizona, wanted to deport all the
invaders and to make their lives so unpleasant "that they
won't even think about doing something that could bring
them back." He succeeded in pairing *immigrant* with
criminal and *invader*, artificially generating feelings of
vulnerability and fear in the non-immigrant community
powerful enough to make people willing, even eager, to
shelter under the protection of police and military — as
if life in a police state were a preferable condition.

Anthropologist Leo Chavez warns us that "Mexicans
of mass destruction" can become a pretext for a military

invasion, for when the border is characterized as a war zone under siege, we can easily slip from war as metaphor to war as practice. Children growing up in such an environment, as psychologist Martín-Baró pointed out, can learn to accept as a given that violence is the way to solve disputes. He called it a "militarization of the mind."

What effects were Sheriff Joe's sweeps having on the children? *Unidos en Arizona,* a human rights organization in Phoenix, was especially worried about the mental health of a little girl whose mother and father were both swept up in a raid. They asked me to evaluate her psychological condition.

The night before I was to see the child, I happened to mention to an Anglo woman in Phoenix that I would be performing a psychological evaluation of a little girl whose parents were in Immigration detention and might be deported to Mexico. She did not ask anything about the child or the parents, but she was quick to say she was glad this was happening. "I hope they take that child away from those criminals and give her to a decent family," she said.

On the day the *Migra* swept their workplace, these so-called "criminals," who the Phoenix woman deemed unfit to be parents, were both at work. Their nine-year-old daughter, Patricia, was waiting for her dad to take her downtown. He'd promised to find an elevator for her so she could touch Braille bumps and know what they felt like. Her curious mind, and her parents' encouragement of her intellectual development, had helped her win Student of the Month three times running the previous year.

Patricia was playing in the yard of the trailer park where the family lived. The TV was on inside and she happened to hear the name of her parents' workplace mentioned by an announcer. She ran inside just in time to see her father on TV, being taken away in handcuffs by the deputies of Joe Arpaio's sheriff's department. She did not have to be told that her mother was being detained too. She knew what a sweep was.

Signs of trauma were clearly present when I sat down with Patricia at her aunt's house. She was a particularly high-functioning child who would be classified as "resilient." But experts on child trauma all agree that resilience has its limits. Children exposed to trauma are changed by it. If it occurs before age eleven, the child is at greater risk of losing trust than if she is older. When it involves loss, the child's sense of vulnerability rises. Research on young children during World War II found that a separation from parents is even more traumatic than exposure to bombs and air raids. During the Contra War of the 1980s, researchers of the Nicaraguan Psychological Association found the same pattern. Patricia was nine. She was separated from both parents. She believed they were in danger.

Many things changed for Patricia the day her parents were taken away. Two months later, though she was safe at the home of an auntie, every time the phone rang she grew frightened, thinking it was the sheriff. She dreamed of people being snatched. She and her playmates now stayed very close to their homes because, as she put it, "We're all scared the sheriff will come and sweep the adults and leave the children alone." She had little appetite, because sitting down to dinner reminded her of the absence of her parents. So did going to the movies, an activity she didn't care for anymore. These "numbing" symptoms serve as protective armor against being flooded by negative emotions, but can result in apathy and withdrawal if they persist. "My mind...*is very big;*" Patricia wrote on an Incomplete Sentences Blank. "I want to know... *how glass is made.*" She had a bright curiosity and enthusiasm for learning. But they were in danger of turning dull.

For some time she had wanted to be a doctor or a teacher when she grew up. She now said she wanted to be a lawyer "because of what happened to my mom and dad — because those people help other people who are in jail." She expressed feelings of hatred toward the sheriff's department. A sketch she made of Sheriff Joe Arpaio was of an ogre you wouldn't want to meet in a dark alley.

The week of our interview, Patricia had learned in catechism about the Christian miracle of the loaves, and she talked about how impressed she was with the cooperative sharing of the bread. The story had touched on one of her personal issues of the moment — the question of whether cooperation and trust were still possible. The Children's Apperception Test, a set of cards with emotionally loaded pictures, gave her an opportunity to display this internal conflict in colors. There was a picture of a tiger, fangs exposed and claws bared, leaping for an unprotected monkey. Her first reaction to the scene was to see it as an arbitrary and cruel aggression. But she was a thoughtful child, and after studying the picture more, she allowed for the possibility that the monkey might have done something to provoke the tiger's anger. Maybe the tiger wasn't the only one at fault. Then she reconsidered again, observing that an aggression like that is natural for a tiger — a hunt for food. And then, wishing to look at this scene from every possible angle, she introduced fatigue to allow for a "time out" in which the tiger could apologize to the monkey, and the monkey, if he did something wrong, could apologize too, and a truce would occur, as a benefit to the entire community. Patricia deftly moved the story from good guy/bad guy simplicity with an abuse of power, to a story of ending violence so that everybody can be happy.

Another Mexican-American child, slightly younger, shown the same card the following day (in his middle-class neighborhood that had not experienced any raids by the sheriff's department), considered only the strategies of the animals, not their motives. He saw the tiger as doing everything possible to catch the monkey, and the monkey everything possible to escape. Finally, the monkey got to a high branch where the tiger couldn't reach him. "The monkey was all safe, and that's the end."

Patricia's conclusion was not so sanguine. Her story ended with a truce, and a truce, unlike a definitive peace treaty, can easily be broken. During a truce the animals may be happy (and perhaps optimistic), but they won't be "all safe." And safety had become a matter of much consequence to Patricia, as it is for all traumatized children.

Safety had become a factor in everything Patricia evaluated, from her father's driving to her situation at school. No child, except one much preoccupied by security, would write as she did on the Incomplete

Sentences Blank, "In school, my teachers…*are nice and safe.*" Her concern for safety stemmed from her personal experience of insecurity. This distinguishes it from the insecurity present in the non-immigrant community, where the fear of criminal invasions through unprotected borders is instilled by propaganda and is entirely lacking in empirical support.

Before the trauma, Patricia was not beset by the doubts that now colored her thoughts about the human condition. Her third-grade teacher had seen her as a person with a talent for conflict resolution: "She helped keep our class community strong," he told me, "and she helped resolve issues and disputes between students."

Conflict resolution is predicated on trust. Now, in fourth grade, Patricia was no longer sure who or what could be trusted — not when there were predators about. Patricia's optimism was on the line. Her parents might be deported. If that happened, she would be reunited with them, but she would lose much of the scaffolding that had supported her sunny outlook until now — her best friend Malena, who had been by her side since kindergarten; her extended family, who were now looking after her and who, she had assured her parents in letters, were taking good care of her while they were in jail; her classmates, a cohort whose stability and consistency contributed much to Patricia's confidence and self-esteem; her school, where she had earned the reputation of outstanding model student; and the self-confidence of her parents, whose own roles as wage-earners and protectors would most likely be compromised if the family were deported to Mexico.

Asked to draw two trees, one planted in Mexico and one in Arizona, Patricia was able to color bright greenery and growth in both trees, indicating that she was not anticipating disaster in a move to Mexico. But the subtle, unconscious indicators of "reaching out to take in the world" represented by the trees' branches, were strong and energetic in the tree growing in Phoenix, and weak, simplified, and impoverished in the tree planted in Mexico. This difference most probably represented Patricia's internalization of what she had been told about her parents' migration history: that in the United States there are opportunities not available in Mexico. On the drawing Patricia was asked to make of any scene she wished, provided it contained a house, a tree, and a person, the house clings to the bottom edge of the paper, a feature associated with insecurity.

Patricia was trying to master the anxieties she felt over the loss of her parents. She tried to comfort her mother and father by sending them pictures of herself, and tried not to despair when she learned that a prison guard saw her picture in her father's cell and took it away. On the Three Wishes Test, where a child of her age and intelligence generally displays an exuberant imagination, her first wish was simply "to have my parents." Her sentence completions and projective tests reflected a struggle to maintain an optimistic view of life and control the anger she felt toward the people responsible for her parents' detention.

On an English language Children's Sentence Completion Test, Patricia responded appropriately to items that pulled for family, such as "My daddy is...*nice and cool;"* "My family is...*the nicest thing ever."* But she also introduced family issues when they were not solicited: "The thing I want to do most of all is...*be with my mom and dad."* "What I want to happen the most is... *to see my parents."* "What I want more than anything is...*my parents."* These references to the separation from her parents were mirrored in the Spanish Incomplete Sentences Blank, where she introduced the following sentiments, rendered here in translation: "At home...*I like to watch television with my mom and dad."* "The best... *is to be with my mother and father, together."* "I suffer... *because they took my mother and my father."* "I need... *my mother and father."* Overall, whether operating in English or in Spanish, Patricia referred to her parents three times more often than would be expected from the prompts alone. There is no question of what problem was responsible for her distress.

Conflicted over how she should feel about authority, Patricia wrote on the Sentences Blank, "People...*are sometimes good and [sometimes] bad."* "I hate...*tigers."* Patricia was being forced to confront the question of whether her own parents were bad people for not having "papers," as the sheriff claimed — whether the monkey might be at fault as well as the tiger. But would this justify her parents being taken from her? Would it justify a forced move to Mexico, a place she'd never known?

Many children of immigrant parents in the United States are having to grapple with these strange dilemmas. An elementary school principal in Phoenix tells of the parent of students at his school, who was stopped for a defective turn signal and turned over to ICE for deportation. "The mother informed me that her sons were devastated upon hearing that their father was incarcerated," he stated. "She and her immediate family spent an extensive amount of time explaining to the boys that their father was not a bad man or a criminal."

In Patricia's case, neither mother nor father was present to do the explaining, and even if she was forced to move to Mexico as those boys were, that could not solve for Patricia the dilemma of guilt and responsibility. The problem could even be exacerbated — by blame being cast on the parents for adjustment difficulties encountered in Mexico after a move. Even school placement has generated adjustment difficulties for deportees, according to the Phoenix school principal, who has stayed in touch with students his school lost to deportation. Though the children are bilingual, they lack the level of Spanish proficiency for age-appropriate placement in Mexico's public schools, and are placed in lower grades with younger students. As when anger turns inward and results in self-destructive acts, anger over an involuntary move, an unfamiliar, possibly hostile environment, and a frustrating school experience can result in acting-out behaviors at home, compromising family unity at precisely the time when the children most need family support.

My psychological evaluation of Patricia closed by summarizing a problem of mental health that was entirely preventable, together with a recommendation for therapy that should never have been needed. In the United States this child of Mexican immigrants had achieved, through her parents' loving attentions and access to public education, a life that was on a trajectory for exemplary success — until the law thrust a tiger into the picture. Struggling with the question of whether the tiger has a right to attack the monkey, she recognized, with the "big mind" given to her by nature and nourished by her parents and teachers, a dilemma that all of us must face but not all of us could articulate as creatively as she did: Is it possible, given separate and opposing needs, for creatures to find a way to live together without destruction?

The System has made a monkey of us. Will we figure out how to avoid being eaten by the tiger?

It took months, but Patricia got her parents back. In time, she will probably regain the trust that got lost in the raid, through her strong alliances in the community fighting for human rights. With others, she marches, speaks out, makes demands for justice, even goes to Washington to advocate for immigration reform. A precocious spokesperson, she has no doubts about the respectability of those parents of hers, those "criminals" that a woman in Phoenix hoped would lose custody of this daughter, who should go to a "good family."

FULL CIRCLE

Harun was detained by the Algerian department for Information and Security four times, and tortured each time before he was let go. They accused him of giving money to a terrorist organization, though he'd never had anything to do with such things. Officially, torture had been outlawed in Algeria, but it continued in practice and was rampant in the military detention center.

When Harun was released for the fourth time, his uncle helped him get a counterfeit French passport, and with that he threaded his way through borders, switching passports as needed, reaching Syria, then Turkey, then the United States. At the airport in Los Angeles, Immigration agents detected the fake document and took him into custody. He insisted his passport was genuine, then admitted it was fake, then asked to apply for political asylum, then began shaking like a leaf and told them never mind. Asked his age, he gave the wrong answer. Some bizarre behavior ensued, and he was hospitalized briefly as a mental patient. Then, with the help of a pro-bono legal agency, he filed an application for political asylum. But he lost. He contradicted himself in court when telling of his many detentions ("four, no three, maybe five") and could not state the dates of when he was tortured. The judge put these inconsistencies together with the use of a phony passport and denied his claim, on the grounds that he was not credible. A psychologist who had examined him in the hospital prepared a summary of his condition, declaring that Harun had Posttraumatic Stress Disorder as a result of having been tortured. But the psychologist's report was not useful for an asylum claim because it failed to point out that a tendency to confuse dates was a frequent concomitant of PTSD, and that Harun had been traveling on a false passport because he was terrified of being recognized as an Algerian.

In the hospital record Harun was identified variously as Asian, Arabic, and Algerian. Someone had written in the box for Patient's Language, "Algerian."

Now Legal Aid was representing him for an appeal of his asylum claim, and his lawyers had arranged for him to be flown to San Francisco, where I was to see him and evaluate his psychological condition, and perhaps discover in this murky picture some mitigating information they could use in the appeal. They had heard that I was good at that sort of thing.

There were signs here of a possible cognitive disorder as well as PTSD resultant from torture. It was also likely that additional problems had built up in consequence of Harun's being hospitalized, jailed, and controlled by people who had no understanding of his past and his culture. I was instructed to meet the Arabic interpreter

at the door of the San Francisco detention facility at ten
a.m. the following Tuesday. Together the interpreter and
I were to pass through jail security and be escorted to
the interview room. If either one of us was late, the jail
might deny us entry.

Of all days to get a late start, why did it have to be
that day? Thinking it would take too long to walk to
the subway, I jumped in the car and drove to the North
Berkeley station of the Bay Area Rapid Transit, BART.
I knew that public transportation was a must for this
trip, because highway traffic on the Oakland-San Francisco Bay Bridge would be heavy, and parking downtown
once I got to the city would cost more than I was being
paid for this gig. I didn't consider that parking at BART
might not be possible, but when I got to the station all
the spots were taken.

I drove on to the Ashby station, but the parking lot
there was completely full, too. This was a problem!
By now it was far too late to think of driving to San
Francisco, but if I was going to get there by train, I had
to get rid of my car. Where to put it? I began circling
the neighborhood, willing to get a ticket for overstaying
a meter, but I could not find a single spot. Nothing!
Finally on a side street I spotted something that was
almost a parking place…really about half a parking place.
If I pulled into that space, the rear end of my car would
jut out into somebody's driveway. But the car that was
parked in the driveway would be able to get out, if it
drove just a little bit over the lawn and sidewalk. I pulled
in and ran up the steps to tell the people I was sorry, it
was an emergency. I rang the bell. No answer. I ran all

the way to BART, and barely got to the appointment on time.

I was so glad it worked out. Over the course of several hours I was able to learn many things that helped explain Harun's inconsistencies. He'd tried to defend the validity of the phony passport because he'd used it to come into the country, and he was terrified of these men in uniform who were interrogating him. For all he knew, these police were in touch with the authorities in Algeria, and would send him back there if they knew that's where he came from.

He told me he was thirty years old, but I saw from his jail ID that he was only twenty-nine. I remarked on that, and the interpreter explained that in Algeria dates of birth are casually identified; it is good enough to come close. He also clued me in on another Algerianism that could lead to a misunderstanding: Harun said he was the third child in his sibling group. That meant he was one of three, *not* the youngest in the group. I wondered how many other cultural pitfalls had prevented this poor man from making himself understood to others.

I saw in Harun some lability of mood and some cognitive slippage. I saw some loose associations. But I didn't see any of the bizarre and uncooperative behavior reported in his hospital records, where he was said to have gone around yelling and acting inappropriately in front of the nurses. He wasn't tearful during our time together, but he admitted to feeling depressed, and he had several physical complaints. He reported feeling suspicious and fearful of other prisoners, one of whom accused him of being an Arab terrorist, another who mocked his dictionary, calling it his Quran. Since religion and prayer were a solace to him, these taunts caused him anxiety with the few things he had available to comfort himself. He felt he was being watched when he prayed, and mistreated by being unable to bathe the number of times required by his religion.

By the time we finished our many hours together, I had no doubt that Harun's confused reports about the number of times he had been detained and tortured, and his contradictions as to which passport he used when traveling to what places, were a product of his trauma and fear, not signs of criminal intent or severe mental illness. Strictly speaking, I did not have "proof" of these matters. I was able to confidently form an opinion based on years of clinical experience. He had passed the subtle tests I used for ruling out malingering, and I was satisfied, on learning about his fantasies and feelings, that he did not harbor antisocial impulses. I had indeed uncovered some information that might prove useful in his asylum appeal: he wasn't a criminal counterfeiter, he was a guy whose life depended on getting by with a phony document.

At four in the afternoon, returning to the place where I'd left the car, I was already braced to see an empty spot where I'd parked it, and resigned to the hassle of locating the car and paying the huge towing and storage fees to get it out. What were these inconveniences compared to *falanga*, a form of torture favored in Algeria? Beating the soles of the feet sends shock waves through the entire nervous system, often resulting in permanent neurological damage. The man I had just interviewed held his arms wrapped around his stomach through most of our time together. He complained that his head hurt terribly, and said his brain had stopped working. Pain in the feet and fingers wouldn't quit, and he couldn't control a jerking in his body. This put some perspective on the nuisance and cost of a towed car.

I turned the corner of the street where I'd parked, and I caught sight of my car. I recognized it by the bumper sticker on the rear end, advertising KPFA, Berkeley's Pacifica network listener-supported radio station. The car was untouched — almost. A note was tucked under the windshield wiper: "You are blocking our driveway. If you do that again, we will have you towed, even if you do support KPFA."

Full of relief, I ran up the steps to thank the kind soul who had spared me so much trouble and money. I rang, and the door opened. And who should be standing there, but the woman who had been Roberto Reyes's girlfriend all those many years ago when I evaluated him for his asylum hearing! What a marvelous coincidence at a moment like this.

Had it not been for that landmark case of her brave boyfriend, who dared to allow a psychological evaluation and then submit it as part of his case for political asylum, I would never have developed an expertise in evaluating people who'd been subjected to torture and other forms of traumatic abuse. Had I not developed that expertise, I would not have been called to see Harun the Algerian. And if it hadn't been for the Algerian I would never have needed a parking place.

PAPI

Patched and wrinkled, the man's pants are dusty from the ride. Rings of sweat turn the armpits of his cotton sleeves a two-tone blue. A straw hat gives him a little protection from the tropical sun beating down on us here at the two-room health post in rural Nicaragua, where he's come on horseback.

Reins in hand, he beckons to me. His other hand clasps the thin, frail waist of the child in front of him in the saddle. She needs a doctor, he explains. For five days she's been coughing, and she isn't getting better. I offer to carry her to the rickety outdoor bench where patients are waiting to be seen. But he hesitates. "I don't have any money," he says.

"I think it's free," I say, though I'm only guessing. I'm just a visitor, a North American health worker stopping to have a look at how they manage out here under austerity, without government support. I stretch out my arms to the semi-conscious little girl who appears to be about eight years old. Her hands curl inward, the contracture of cerebral palsy. A gurgle of a cough escapes her dry lips.

"My daughter's an invalid," he says, "since birth, she can't walk."

"It's all right, I can carry her," I say, and he passes her down to me and then dismounts, hitching the horse to a barbed wire fence across the rutted road.

A mother on the bench nurses a baby. A little boy with a patch on his eye plays with a stick. I sit down with the girl on my lap, while her father nods to the other waiting patients as he goes inside to see about a doctor.

A few minutes later he comes back and takes his daughter from me, and we exchange a few friendly words. I stare in awe when I learn that Rosita, this tiny wraith of a child, is not eight, but fourteen. I want to memorize this man's round face and intense brown eyes, his calloused hands tenderly embracing the little girl, and his expressive mouth that has just attested to a minor miracle, yet with a voice so humble and soft as to deny that anything wondrous has been revealed. How many parents have I known in my lifetime? Hundreds? Thousands? Caring, doting, strict, indulgent, neglectful, abusive... From the prideful parent-of-the-month to the monster mother of Munchausen, I thought I'd seen them all. But I could never have imagined what I see before me now. Here is a man who, deep in the volcanic *campo* of Nicaragua, without electricity, without medicine or running water, without telephones or lights or toys or books or bathrooms or doctors, has kept his severely disabled child alive for fourteen years. I'd never known another soul who could have done that.

"And Death Shall Have No Dominion," I think, remembering Dylan Thomas's insistent prayer.

At a loss for what to say, I pat Rosita on the hand. "Does she speak?" I ask.

He smiles modestly. "Only one word," he whispers. "Papi."

LIKE A SNAKE

EVERYBODY STOPS TO LISTEN: BROKEN GLASS rattling in tin barrels? An explosion of ice cubes? Hail battering cars in the parking lot?

A huge commotion on the outskirts of San Salvador at nightfall. A pupusa vendor stops turning her *masa* from one palm to the other. She dabs her fingers in water, wipes them on her oversized tee-shirt, and shakes her head: "*Loros!*"

Loros? Parrots?

She's right. It's the angry screeching of a thousand homeless parrots scolding two rolling bulldozers that are paving the way for Westinghouse and Wendy's. The corporations are having a party where the parrots used to have a forest.

A shopping mall? In this poor country where more than half the population lives in poverty? I shake my head, too.

The rest of the night sounds come in whispers — the soft groans of frogs; insects humming as they change shifts: mosquitoes that carry dengue work days, the ones that carry malaria work nights. I wonder if the pupusa vendor has a mosquito net.

In the morning we're back on the road, sniffing the fresh aromas of the lush greenery and watching the ribbon of smoke from a distant volcano. At the edge of a small village I stop to stretch. My hand is on my forehead to shade my eyes from the blinding tropical sun as I try to make out the inscription on a monument across the road. Close by, a man in Levi's and work shirt is buying mangoes at a covered pushcart. He finishes, adjusts the brim of his straw hat, and walks in my direction, followed by a slow-moving, bent-tailed dog.

I look at my watch, guessing we'll reach the Honduran border around noon, in about an hour. Over in Honduras, the Resistance has hopes of restoring democracy to their beleaguered country, to undo the damage of the coup that overthrew their elected president. Here in El Salvador, people worry that U.S. manipulation of the political process will further impoverish the poor. The economy is so bad that many families depend on remittances sent by relatives in the United States. U.S. money financed the shopping mall, too, the one the parrots are complaining about.

The man who bought the mangoes stops by my side and smiles. He tells me the inscription is a tribute to Oscar Romero, and he deciphers for me the words on the marble base, "an old saying that Monsignor Romero liked to quote — and it's the truth, too":

THE LAW IS LIKE A SNAKE:
IT ONLY BITES THOSE WHO GO BAREFOOT.

"A good saying," I agree, "*un buen dicho.*"

Central Americans are pleased that Pope Francis has beatified the martyred Archbishop, paving the way to make official the sainthood already conferred upon him by the people. "San Romero was a great man," I remark.

Watching the old dog meander toward a distant shack where a bed sheet and two pairs of pants hang on a clothesline, the man asks where I come from.

"California," I say.

He mentions that he has two sons in San Francisco.

"*Really!*" Neighbors! I live right across the Bay. "What do they do there?"

"They go to school," he says.

This is a great surprise. Even to get through grade school in a poor rural village like this is a tremendous achievement. Education abroad? Almost a miracle. And there are two of them!

"You're from here?" I ask.

He nods and points out beyond the shack where the old dog has gone, up a narrow dirt trail that leads to a cluster of small wooden houses with tin roofs. There is no electric line. "Right over there," he says.

"And your sons in San Francisco, they're… ?" I don't know how to ask this. I'm wondering if they could have been among the droves of unaccompanied minors fleeing violence from the gangs and corrupt police, hopping the northbound freight train, the treacherous *bestia*…

"They go to Mission High School," he offers. I hear a reproach in his voice, though only a moment ago he'd been warm and friendly. There's something I'm not understanding.

He looks again at the statue, and then fixes his dark brown eyes on me. "They've lived there all their life. They were born at San Francisco General Hospital."

"Oh."

I said it as if that explained everything, but in fact I'm confused. The bleak village, the rickety fruit stand, the unlikely monument with its pithy message, the U.S. citizen kids in San Francisco, and dad out here in the *campo* of El Salvador, buying two mangoes at a time...

A flock of parrots passes overhead, flying toward the monument. The man bows his head, then looks away to the north with an expression of great sadness. In a choked voice, he explains: "I was deported twelve years ago."

TREATMENT OF CHOICE: BASEBALL

It was the season of the winds. Hurricane Mitch had ripped through Nicaragua and torn off the first piece of the Casitas Volcano above Posoltega. With a deafening churning and trembling that survivors described as the sound of helicopters from hell, the land slid down the mountainside, stopping only when its own massive tonnage dammed it up after two kilometers. A torrential rain that had been pouring for nearly two weeks kept pounding its water into the earth, until the colossal weight of the saturated mountain smashed through the dam and brought down the entire land mass: earth, rocks, mud, branches, trees, and houses. Panicked humans and animals careened through the torrent in a jumbled, churning, cataclysmic chaos the survivors called *el corriente.*

When it finally stopped, people crawled out from crazy, impossible places like treetops and rooftops, or they remained crushed in the rocky debris where they died quickly, or sometimes slowly. Whole villages were buried under its mud, like Rolando Rodriguez, a settlement named for a man who had fought for the right of camp-esinos to own this poor, unstable land. El Porvenir was buried too, the village whose name means "The Future."

The campesinos who lived in these villages high on the Casitas Volcano were now landless again, and homeless, bereft of all possessions. Traumatized and depressed, they camped on the floors of local school buildings, eating food trucked in by relief agencies.

The doctors and nurses of our international team of health workers were vaccinating survivors and monitoring sanitary and nutrition needs. I'm just a psychologist, and wasn't sure I had anything to offer. I sat down on a little stone wall, next to a man in his thirties, and introduced myself.

Santiago saw combat as a Sandinista soldier fighting the Contras, but said he'd never in his life seen anything to compare with this. His wife and both his children were lost to the *corriente*.

Where would he go? Probably back up there to his parcel, he says, glancing at the huge scar on the moun-tainside above us. The government had confiscated it, declaring the Casitas Volcano unsafe for anything but a park. But that was no geology lesson, Santiago said; it was a land-grab.

"You really think the land can be trusted?" His faith in the mountain reminded me of a woman who gets beat up by her husband but wants to go back 'cause he won't do it again. I told him that. He surprised me with a laugh. Then he told me quietly, humbly, that farming was the only thing he'd ever known. "I'm good at it," he said. "And I don't have any other talents."

He was able to laugh, he looked to the future: there were strengths here. I gave him a doubtful look. "A man like you? Just one skill? That's hard to believe." (I was using my years to advantage. I can pull off a remark like that without being taken for a flirt).

Santiago admitted to me with a shy smile that he's actually pretty good at baseball.

"The kids are bored; they need somebody to start them playing and keep them from getting too depressed. How about organizing a baseball game?" I thought an activity like that would be therapeutic for both the coach and the players. The day before, at another makeshift shelter without guitar, radio, or music, I'd organized some little girls into a chorus, to put on a show for the grownups. Same principle.

"There's just two problems with your suggestion," he said.

"Oh?"

"No ball. And no bat."

Small wonder, I thought, when the bare necessities of life — a towel, a mattress, a change of clothes, a toothbrush — were also lacking. But this was a man who supported a family by farming on a poor, eroded, steep mountainside that geologists had identified as one of the most vulnerable spots in the country. He knew how to get by on very little; his reference point was a sandlot, not Yankee Stadium. Maybe we could improvise.

"So where can you get a ball and bat?" I asked.

"Maybe from the national team, but I don't know anybody."

"Look," I said, "I'm not from here, and I don't even know too much about baseball. But I remember that Sergio Ramirez, the Vice-President during the Sandinistas, wrote a great story called 'The Perfect Game,' and another called 'The Centerfielder.' Don't you think he'd help?"

Santiago looked me over. He knew one of the stories, has maybe heard of the other one.

He of course knew that Sergio Ramirez cared about baseball. I could see my credibility rising. "Can you write him a letter?" One can ask a Nicaraguan a question like that. The literacy campaign of the Sandinista revolution was so successful that even people in the most remote regions of the country learned to read and write.

✳✳✳

I left for Managua, taking with me Santiago's letter to Sergio Ramirez. Before I could mail it, I ran into David, a Canadian nurse on his way to Posoltega. I pressed into his palm a twenty dollar bill that had been pressed into my own hand by a colleague in California, for an unspecified "something that's really needed."

"Look," I said, "There's this refugee camp up there, where they really need a ball and bat. There's a guy there named Santiago..." I didn't have to go into it too much. David had been providing health care in Nicaragua; he understood how baseball can become a treatment of choice.

David scoured the markets in León and found a bat and four balls. And then he found Santiago.

He wrote to me, describing how Santiago's face lit up when he saw the surprise.

Maybe this wasn't an out-of-the-park home run, but it definitely counted as a solid base hit. We'd helped put a runner on.

FICTION,
THE HARD WAY

SUNSHINE

YOU NEVER TOLD ME, JACK, WHEN I PORED THROUGH
a collection of your stories after winning the Jack London
Prize, that I'd be thinking of you on a freezing sand
bank, ass in the air, trying to get a spark out of dry sticks.
"To Build a Fire" had held me spellbound. Now it held
me hostage with two pieces of lukewarm tinder that
weren't going to heat up no matter how hard I rubbed.
Damn you, Jack, and Bradbury too, with his *Fahrenheit
451*. Thoreau, too: that thing about firewood warming
you twice, first when you chop it, then when you burn
it. Damn you all, and damn the memories fluttering
through my addled mind like snippets dropped by
Tobias Wolff's guy in the bank heist. All was literature
now — stories, books, essays, and the novel I was writing,
the worthless, dripping piece of junk on the sand bank
behind me.

For hours I'd scraped, climbed, and ducked my
way through tangled brush in the clogged stream that
I thought was the South Fork of the Tuolumne River.

Purple tote bag slung over shoulder, I'd left camp a happy writer, telling my friend Penny I'd be back at six, and I'd walked about a mile to a spot where I traipsed around with the butterflies and then went rock hopping up-river to look for a sunny rock where I could kick back and take out my red pencil for the fiftieth rewrite of the novel stuffed in the tote bag. The manuscript was supposed to get me to an agent, who would get me to a publisher, who would get me into print as a fiction writer and save me from anonymity. Ah, the literati's illusions, the things they never taught you about the writer's life...

After a while, rock hopping became the only route because when I tried to go by land, the thicket at the banks of the stream drew blood from my sleeveless arms and stuck branches and thorns into my uncovered legs. So I picked my way stone by river stone, until a huge tree sprawled bank to bank, demanding a clamber over its massive trunk lying dead in the water. Using the stubs of its broken limbs as ladder rungs, I got to the top and gingerly reached down the other side. The tree dropped me feet-first into a shallow stone-strewn pool where, canvas bag aloft, I was able to wade for a time, manuscript safe in the air and feet steady in the water, moving along the river bed in quest of a shoreline writing spot — or at least a trail, any trail, to deliver me from the water.

In front of me, the way was blocked by a forest of water plants growing from the cracks in river boulders. I had to make it past this, too. Probably, I figured, this was stage two of the chaotic wood-and-leaf mass that formed the dam I'd seen earlier — before the downstream trail veered inland and I lost sight of the river. It seemed that the chaos wasn't a one-shot deal, but was more like an ongoing siege on the waterway. Enormous round leaves, one per stem, sat atop their long stalks like open umbrellas, stretching in clumps across the river, blocking my way, hiding what lay ahead. Dozens of them, hundreds of them, gangs of green umbrellas stealing my vision and defending their liquid turf. I pushed against them, through them, past them, only to find more and more of them as my wet sneakers hunted on their liquid jungle floor for stones to support my feet, away from the rivulets of waterfall that made everything slippery. Only when I had a secure footing could I let go of the fistfuls of brittle plant stems I clutched for balance, and then I could move forward, rock to boulder to ankle-deep river, to more umbrella thugs and tree trunk barricades to find a trail.

It had to be here somewhere. My famously poor sense of direction was no handicap this time. I knew the difference between upstream and downstream, and the laws of nature said that going up would get me back. I'd followed a trail downstream, for a ways beyond where the path split off from the river, and I'd flitted with the butterflies through a field teeming with ladybugs, then fought through the jumble and started on this slow rock-hopping trek in what was obviously a very twisty river. Soon there had to be a trail, and beyond that, the camp. Between the two, if I was lucky, there would be a comfortable spot to work on the manuscript. Years before, when I was writing introductions for essays by Martín-Baró, I'd discovered forests and riverbanks as the premier places to work without distraction. "Aren't you scared?" people would say. "A woman going off by yourself like that?" Scared! It never crossed my mind. While Martín-Baró was writing those essays, the Salvadoran soldiers who later killed him prowled around outside his office window. *That's* scary.

Around the bend up ahead I could see an eroded hillside, sign of a trail for sure. But getting there would require some tricky bouldering and major battles with the umbrellas, and I'd already fallen three times, knocking bare knees and vulnerable elbows into the unforgiving walls of granite boulders. Occupied with thoughts of safety, I forgot to watch my feet. Before I knew what was happening, a fourth fall dumped me sideways into the river, washing the tops of my thighs through the water. No time to move the purple bag. Its lower edge turned black from the wet. Frantically I pulled the paper from the sack as soon as I got my footing. Dry! The manuscript was all dry except for the bottom margin. What luck! Never mind that everything not covered by my simple summer clothing was a scratchy mess of scraped and bleeding skin; eight- and-a-half by ten inches of my passport to the future was unharmed! The unexpected splash into the water brought home to me, though, how treacherous this country was; I'm not usually a faller.

The eroded hillside up ahead seemed to have sunshine at the crest where the trail cut through, so I beached again and thrashed through a tangle of blackberry vines to get to it. It was not easy going. Nearly an hour must have passed before I was close enough to the top to read the bad news that sometimes an escarpment is only an escarpment and not an advertisement for a road. But an acre of sweet berries in a California forest, I knew, is nearly always the garden setting for a bear's outdoor café. I'd been helping myself to berries as I smashed through the heavy brush, sort of the way the bears break into our cars to help themselves to our lunch. Was some furry thing going to come after me for stealing? I beat it down the hill.

Sorry for all the time I'd lost, I plodded on upstream, though I gave more than a moment's thought to reversing course and heading back the way I'd come, through the boulders, downed trees, slippery rocks, and umbrella monsters. My banged up arms and legs begged me not to put them through all that again. I yielded to their pleas. Onward!

There were no signs of recent human life in this wilderness. None. I'd seen a rusty cable around a big lodgepole pine, left over from logging days some eighty years ago, and near it an old drum, same vintage, that once held Mark's Chocolate Icing. I'd smiled at that, Mark being my favorite man and chocolate my favorite flavor, but these old relics also brought on a lonely awareness of how far I'd traveled from phone reception, roads, trails, anything to connect me to the people I cared about. What if I were to die out here? Nobody would ever find me. What if my birthday, coming in a few days, were to wind up being my death day? No, that was absurd. I wasn't going to die out here. Up ahead I was going to find a trail to take me straight to the edge of the camp. I probably wouldn't get much writing in today, I'd been out here so long. All these obstructions and detours had kept me trekking through this meandering river for a good five or six hours.

The next bend exposed a beautiful granite cliff over a chunk of solid rock as big as a flat-roofed house. Early on I'd been seeing boulders as smooth as ducks, as big as elephants, as round as a turtle or flat as a whale's back, but ever since that feeling of loneliness had draped itself over me, my metaphors, as if traumatized by the absence of humanity, shied away from nature and led my searching eyes to things that people use — refrigerators, Volkswagons, coffee tables, houses. Once, I saw what looked like a bright yellow flashlight that someone had lost in a pile of rocks under a dead tree. I grew so excited at the prospect of a careless hiker being close by that I almost wept when I got near enough to see it was a colorful shelf fungus. A dented beer can would have been a joy.

I contemplated going up to visit that gorgeous hunk of granite shaped like a house, but it required a technical climb of the sort I hadn't done in more than thirty years, and never without ropes and an upper belay. Caution said no. The river, though, had other ideas; there was no way to continue forward unless I went up there. A dam of clogged boulders and branches in the water had formed a pool so deep that I'd have to swim it, and a swim would soak the manuscript. I had to go for a land traverse.

On the huge ridge, reached by arduous maneuvers of pressure holds and finger grips, I was rewarded by a true sign of human life. So what if it was a thousand years old? This Native American *metate* used for grinding edible plants told a story of a time when the river flowed clear and a friend from long ago sat as I was sitting: safe, warm, happy, in love with the view. I ate a piece of French toast I'd set aside from breakfast, saving the other for later, and I washed down half my ounce-and-a-half box of raisins with the river water I'd been drinking all day from a plastic bottle. There were warnings back at camp about parasites in the water, but parasites are curable, I figured; death isn't. The woozy-headed, stumble-footed jig of dehydration could be fatal in a situation like this.

It was three o'clock. I had traveled for miles, for hours, a cartoon version of the Haitian proverb: *Beyond the mountains, more mountains.* Where was I? Penny was expecting me back at six. If I turned back to struggle through the morass that brought me here, I'd never get there in time. If I pushed on upstream, I was bound to get to the camp, and it couldn't be much farther.

After the rest on the happy ridge, I pushed on through the water, dodging umbrellas, crossing logs, climbing boulders, and falling — falling on slippery rocks, falling from algae-coated sloping banks, falling from ledges and logs, falling in the umbrella leaves, in the rivulets, in the river, in shallow trickles and deep pools, falling completely submerged, manuscript and all, in the never-ending, never-clearing stream that I later learned was not the Tuolumne River, but something called Soldier Creek, taking me deeper and deeper into this impenetrable wilderness. Way back by the butterflies there'd been a confluence of streams, but I hadn't known that. I'd seen water flowing, and followed it upstream.

At six-thirty I spotted a sand bank and climbed out. I had another hour of daylight, but I'd fallen twenty-one times.

I looked around, thankful for a stretch of land without brambles.

That's fresh bear tracks, said the intellectual in my head.

Bears don't want to hurt you, said the writer.

You stole the berries.

Bears don't know from stealing.

Think claws.

Think Goldilocks.

The voices in my head argued over the risks of camping so close to what might be a bear's lair, and finally came to a TINA truce: There Is No Alternative. The terrain hadn't changed over the last couple of hours, but I had. I was depleted of energy and sore all over. My judgment was shot. If a fall into a boulder knocked me out, that could be the end of me. Footprints or no, I would have to spend the night in this desolate place.

I rubbed my sticks and cursed the writers. Hanging my stash of bread and raisins in a tree as an offering to the animals, I gathered long branches for a shelter. Enough to break the wind if it came up, and hold in a little body heat, the three-sided wood structure wasn't much good for anything else except as a message to the bear: This isn't a bear kind of thing — please don't disturb.

You think that makes sense?

You don't?

I thatched the roof with those wicked umbrella plants, though that meant having to wade back into the river to fetch them, and it was already getting cold. I'd decided those umbrella thugs weren't killers after all, just accomplices — the guys who hid the body when the homicidal boulders finished you off.

DUSK

Cold and wet, I sat down in the sand next to my house of sticks to review my assets. No serious injuries, that was a plus. A face-first crash into a boulder hadn't broken my nose, hadn't caused a nosebleed, didn't even hurt. My game leg was holding up, and the wounds on my lacerated arms and legs weren't dirty, no sign of infection. Add in the wristwatch that hadn't stopped running despite total submersion over and over, and the sum was good news.

Food? I glanced at the tree in my front yard, its cache hanging down like a clump of bananas. Bears are messy, there might be a few leftover raisins after a raid. And I had water galore. I wasn't going to go looney from dehydration.

What'd you say?

Nothing, forget it.

Healthy and in good shape, I wasn't going to die of exposure from a single night in the woods, even if all I had covering me was a sleeveless tee shirt and a pair of shorts. I had a toy flashlight half the size of my thumb; I knew how to signal an SOS in case an airplane flew over. I had a friend who would start to miss me pretty soon and maybe tell somebody. I had a pocket knife.

Aron Ralston.

Oh, God.

Jack London himself could not have thought up *Between a Rock and a Hard Place*, Ralston's true story of a solo climb in Utah, where he got trapped by a falling boulder that hopelessly wedged his arm in the rock. Ralston saved his own life by cutting off the arm — with a dull pocketknife.

But he got out alive, I said to myself — take heart! A moment later a song started up in my head, a corny show tune from the fifties that I'd never liked, never sung, never realized was on deposit in my memory bank: "In the cool cool cool of the evening, tell 'em I'll be there..." The infernal tune had been taking over my brain for the last few hours, exactly the way an equally obnoxious song took over Ralston's while he was prisoner to the boulder. Why were we haunted by these horrid sounds? Oliver Sacks...didn't I remember something about one of his patients who couldn't get rid of "Easter Parade" blaring through the radio in her head? She was stuck too, as I recalled — in a convalescent home. Was audio punishment the fate of people who were trapped? Sacks had talked about musical epilepsy, seizures in the frontal lobes. I should pay attention to this queer symptom, try to document it for science. But that was not possible, because all I was able to think when I tried to focus on science, was "In the cool cool cool of the evening, better bring a chair." Bring a chair? Not likely. Probably "save a chair." Yes, "save a chair." Or was it "grab a chair"?

Was I really out here in the setting sun, sitting next to a house of sticks on a piece of property owned by a bear, debating the lyrics of a stupid song? Was I losing it? I forced myself to get back to basics: how to make it through the coming night when I was already shivering. No jacket. No cover for my battered arms and legs. Wet shorts, wet t-shirt, wet manuscript in a wet canvas bag. Using my raw elbows as anchors, I scooted into my three-sided shelter and worked out a plan: no looking at watch, that would be too depressing; no peeing in bed, despite the wet — too gross. At the crack of dawn get up and *go back* — the only sure way to reach civilization. Meanwhile, keep flashlight at the ready in case an airplane flies by.

Here just outside Yosemite National Park, wildfires had been raging all summer. If only I'd had matches, I could have safely built a fire and a smoke spotter would have seen it and sent people right away. Possibly they were patrolling right now, content that in my neck of the woods the red dragon was asleep; unaware of a stranded writer who would not sleep at all, who would stare into the ghostly night thinking she'd gladly trade a lifetime of royalties for the touch of a human hand, the sound of a human voice. Mailer had called his book on writing *The Spooky Art*. Little did he know.

The bear's fresh paw prints were only steps away from my shaking body. Having recently read Temple Grandin's *Animals in Translation*, I asked myself: How does a bear feel? How does he think? Grandin's deep sensitivity to our animal cousins brought comfort to my troubled mind. It showed me how to think of the bear as my friend, as someone who would understand that I meant no harm, as one of the benevolent forest creatures like the ones in the fairy tales who had helped Hansel and Gretel. If there were eyes upon me in these dark woods, they were most likely friendly eyes.

You believe that?

I believe it.

On what grounds?

Logic was toughing out another round against Faith when the referee stopped the fight to make way for a quartet coming through from Tin Pan Alley, tickling the needles of the overhanging conifers and rattling my tired brain with yet another soppy crooning of "In the cool cool cool of the evening, tell'em I'll be there..."

In my windy shelter I lay shaking in the frigid night, cold to the bone, more alone than I'd ever imagined possible. If morning ever came, it would be September 1, an eerie date, a strange coincidence, as Auden had a 1939 poem by that name, with lines so uncanny that my freezing, bloodstained arms lurched with violent spasms as I recalled them: *The music must always play... Lost in a haunted wood... Defenseless under the night...*

Auden was writing of one war; I, awake and shivering, began thinking of another one. Isolation, sleep deprivation, and miserably low temperatures were three forms of torture my country was using in its war on terrorism: at Guantánamo Bay, at Baghram and Abu Ghraib, and in black sites all over the earth — against prisoners defenseless under the night. My suffering, I knew, was no match to theirs. My wet from a high Sierra stream was not the same as the piss of a prison guard on your face. The drowning of my novel was not the same as having to watch your holy scriptures flushed down a filthy toilet. I, blinking my pathetic SOS at the gloomy sky, knew that if my signal was seen, people would come to help me. The prisoners, in the jaws of cruelty, believed what their torturers screamed during hours of interrogation: Nobody can hear you, nobody knows where you are, you'll never get out of here alive. For me, there was every confidence in the world that once people knew I was lost, they would mount a rescue. Auden again: *We must love one another or die.*

So I might survive. And the novel? I contemplated the inky words dripping down the pages of my ravaged manuscript. There were other writers who knew the sorrow I was feeling. Not too many years ago, Maxine Hong Kingston lost an entire book in the Oakland Hills fire; she was left with mere ashes. The protagonist in an Isaac Singer story, a writer, lost his manuscript somewhere in Buenos Aires and was left with nothing at all. And me? What did I have? I had three hundred waterlogged pages in a soaking wet canvas bag. Shit.

Get real, said the intellectual. *What matters here is your survival, period.*

But all that work, said the writer. *All those drowned phrases, gone.*

Suddenly a light switched on in my house of sticks. Those pages! They weren't burned to a crisp. They weren't disappeared in a strange city. They were right here, in the bag, tangible — maybe not salvageable the way a terrible first draft is salvageable, but weren't they good for *something?* Paper! Orwell had covered himself with paper to keep warm when he was down and out in Paris and London. Bettelheim had written about prisoners slipping somebody a piece of newspaper in the concentration camp, to put under a threadbare jacket. Paper! Was it like goose down, losing its insulating properties when it got wet? Or was it like wool, continuing to give protection even when drenched with water? The canvas bag was under my head, being used as a pillow.

With fingers stiff from the cold, I removed the bag of sodden manuscript from its pillow position. I set it over my heart, an eight-and-a-half by eleven-inch trial blanket. I was shaking and shuddering from the cold, but I held it in place. I waited, and... it was almost unbelievable!

In the cool cool cool of the evening, I felt the chill leaving my left breast. It was working! I moved the tepid cover to my right shoulder for a while, and later to my hip, and to my battered right leg. Left leg. Right arm below the gash. Left arm above the lacerated elbow. It was the Yosemite Hokey Pokey, danced all through the night, warming up each and every part of my poor, lonesome, freezing self, eight-and-a-half by eleven inches at a time, choreographed by my precious, ravaged, illegible manuscript. I trembled through the long and sleepless night, finding comfort in the blurry words that lay so close to my heart.

DAWN

It's light out.

Now what?

During a fierce argument with myself about turning back versus plodding on, interrupted by more refrains of the idiotic song, I calculated that, subtracting the climb up to the granite house and the thrash up the escarpment, six hours should get me to the ladybugs, and the ladybugs meant certain safety, whereas the upstream direction could go on for a thousand miles, all the way to the Continental Divide.

I would go back, but I would have to be very, very careful, lest a fall knock me unconscious and sink me in a watery grave under the umbrellas. Those umbrella thugs mustered in green camouflage across the river scared me more than the elusive bear who never showed himself. They were the wilderness contingent of the CIA's rendition squads: ready to strike, to turn me into one of the disappeared and make me equal after all to the prisoners rotting incognito in undisclosed locations. If the umbrella thugs had their way, the people who cared about me, like the ones who cared about the languishing detainees, would be left in a morbid limbo, never knowing if I was alive or dead. It was for those loved ones, my family and friends, that I staggered, climbed, swam, and swayed my way through the crooked stream, ignoring the raw scrapes on my knees and elbows, the dozens of cuts and scratches all over my thighs, shins, and arms, and the pain a bruised tailbone inserted into every uncertain step. I was in worse shape than the evening before, weak from lack of sleep and too little food. This was going to be a longer trip back than I thought.

Seven hours into the bouldering, climbing, and stumbling, when falling had become a way of life and survival an iffy proposition, I rested on a sun-drenched rock wedged in the riverbank, and took a drink of water. Up ahead, one of yesterday's most difficult boulders, easy to swim around but treacherous to ascend, glistened in the sunlight. I remembered reaching its peak and having to straddle a wide gap to get to a place where I could work my way down without the manuscript getting wet. Suddenly that challenge struck me as hilarious. I started laughing at the folly of it — all those river gymnastics, those daring leaps and heart-stopping slips, to protect a piece of fiction! *Fiction!* Could anything be more ridiculous? And it got saturated anyway! Who *cares* if the novel is ever finished? What difference does it make if it's published? *Fiction!* A treatise on the insulating properties of paper, or a passionate reflection on the courage of Martín-Baró, or the nastiness of umbrella gangs — those would be worth risking your life for! But *fiction?* I was giddy with surprise at my own silliness. I sat on the rock, staring at my past and my future, laughing, laughing, laughing at the absurdity of it all.

I was still laughing when I heard the gritty *thunks* of the chopper.

Without a thought to falling, I leapt from the rock to the middle of the river and waved my red hat as a flag, ferociously, like a patriot gone mad. Laughing still, I put the flag on the end of a long stick so the helicopter would see me for sure if it came back. I laughed at my own absurdity and at the joy of being found, as the helicopter circled above me three times, four times, leaving no doubt that I'd been seen.

I sat and waited, and after a time — how long? I couldn't say; time had ceased to exist — I heard my name being called. Saved!

All the way back to camp, wrist-to-wrist with the members of the volunteer search party who had come from all over the state to hunt for me, I berated myself for my folly. They had thrashed through the cruel brush and stumbled on the slippery rocks to get me, a foolish fiction writer. They had talked to my son on the phone, been in radio contact with the helicopter, and told all the people at camp that they could relax and call off their ad hoc search teams. They had notified the sheriff at Rescue Central to say that the ultraviolet night flights wouldn't be needed, and promised Mark he did not have to organize a memorial for a dead girlfriend.

Through the trek out of the forest, and all during the highway ride to the camp, my mind was fixed on the foolishness of my sacrifice. All that...for *fiction?*

Only when my sluggish brain cells began to absorb how extensive the mobilization had been and how many people were celebrating my rescue, did my grudge against fiction begin its retreat back to the lunatic place it had come from. A chair covered with a confusion of confetti sat waiting for me in the cool cool cool of the evening, and I was able to collect my thoughts.

Jack London, I declared when the air finally cleared, this survivor is going back to work on that book, that novel, that work of...yes, fiction. To finish it, even if she has to start all over and scratch it out on sheets of tree bark. Because literature is worth more than the paper it is written on, and good fiction, like a good life, speaks to truth — the truth of our existence as social beings. Auden got it right: *We must love one another or die.*

Human Rights and Wrongs

Reluctant Heroes Fight Tyranny

2017

ADRIANNE ARON

PRIZE WINNER ◆ ESSAY COLLECTION

ADRIANNE ARON, PH.D.

A PRACTICING PSYCHOLOGIST IN BERKELEY, CALIFORNIA, Dr. Adrianne Aron was for many years clinical director of a pro-bono service for Central American refugees, the Centro Ignacio Martín-Baró, a project of the Committee for Health Rights in the Americas. She is the co-editor and chief translator of a collection of essays by Martín-Baró, *Writings for a Liberation Psychology* (Harvard University Press, 1994, 1996) and translator (with Introduction) of Mario Benedetti's compelling drama, *Pedro y el Capitán*, into English as *Pedro and the Captain* (Cadmus Editions, 2009). She is the author of several articles and book chapters in psychology, and many short pieces of creative prose. For respite from her long hours with traumatized refugees she took up writing fiction and little essays of creative nonfiction, and, on receiving awards in both genres, was encouraged to write Human Rights and Wrongs in the style of a collection of stories. Her website is www.adriannearon.com.

Writings for a Liberation Psychology

HARVARD UNIVERSITY PRESS, 1994

Co-editor, chief translator, and author of introductions for this collection of essays by Ignacio Martín-Baró.

Pedro and the Captain

CADMUS EDITIONS, 2009

Translator from the Spanish of Mario Benedetti's Pedro y el Capitán and author of the Introduction.

PUBLICATION ACKNOWLEDGMENTS

"The Best Paid Psychologist in America" was published in *Anastamos*, 4, 2017. Parts of this chapter originally appeared in "Applications of Psychology to the Assessment of Refugees Seeking Political Asylum," *Applied Psychology: An International Review*, 1992, 41 (1): 77-91.

"The Drunken Fog of Ernesto Cruz" was first published by *Reed*, Issue 67, 2014.

"Fiction, the Hard Way" was awarded *Adventum's* Ridge to River Prize, and published in the magazine's debut issue, 2011.

USA Dishonor and Disrespect (Haitian Interdiction 1981-19__), 1991
Linoleum block print on a seven-color lithograph printed on moldmade Okawara paper
Artist: Eric Avery • Collaborating printer: Mark Attwood • Published by Tamarind Institute
46½"x 34" • Edition: 30

Eric Avery's powerful linoleum block print, "USA Dishonor and Disrespect (Haitian Interdiction 1981-1994)," appropriates John Singleton Copley's 1778 painting, "Watson and the Shark," which depicts the incident in Havana harbor when Brook Watson, a boy of 14, lost a leg to a shark. Avery's 1991 work was created in a context of ongoing bloodletting in the Caribbean waters. A news release of the U.S. Committee for Refugees in July, 1990 tells it succinctly: HAITIANS DIE AT SEA, VICTIMS OF INHUMANE INTERDICTION POLICIES. In the nine years prior to that release, from the time that the U.S. began a program to specifically target Haitian migrants, 21,361 Haitians had been interdicted by the U.S. Coast Guard, and only eight persons were allowed ashore to pursue asylum claims. There were also interdiction-related deaths. The 1990 headline for example, refers to the drowning of 39 Haitians after their boat was interdicted by the Bahamian Defense Force.

Roger Winter, USCR Director, appealed to Bahamian authorities, as he'd appealed numerous times to the U.S. government, to stop the interdictions. Winter states: "As long as the United States gives higher priority to pushing the unwanted away from our shores than saving their lives, ... asylum seekers will continue to drift — alone and forsaken — on unforgiving seas."

On Eric Avery's website (DocArt.com), Print Catalog 1991 includes more information about the egregious treatment of Haitians by the USA and also presents the historical source — Copley's "Watson and the Shark" — for the scene portrayed in Avery's contemporary contextualization appearing on this book's cover.

THE FUTURE IS UP FOR GRABS,
CONCEIVED BY THE IMAGINATION,
CONSTRUCTED WITH WORDS, AND
EXPLAINED AS A STORY.

SUNSHOT ꗒ P R E S S

Bloodshot Stories

by Jeff P. Jones

You want it darker? Jeff P. Jones carries on in the trajectory that runs from Kafka through Philip K. Dick to Cormac McCarthy (with a sprinkling of John Barth thrown in). Whether inviting the reader to comb through the dank stacks of a Stalin archive, or sweat inside the soldered-closed cab of a post-apocalyptic dump truck, or become an atom splitting from the inside, or a single brain dispersing into the universe — these brilliantly researched and deeply imagined stories are never the expected. A stunning collection.

—Janet Burroway

Author of *Writing Fiction: A Guide to Narrative Craft* (9th edition)

SUNSHOT PRESS

Shot In The Head

by Lee Varon

Lee Varon's poems take us to the shooting of her grandfather in 1936. The images like "a blush that turned to blood," are breath-taking. At first it is a family story, but as you examine it further, the views of prejudice in the community are jaw-dropping, yet amazingly relevant to today's issues. Her grandmother, Virginia Marie, navigates life with pride and loyalty, yet fear and bigotry, highlighting the complexity of human nature.

—Jean Flanagan

Author of *Black Lightning*

SUNSHOT PRESS

An Incomplete List of My Wishes

by Jendi Reiter

Jendi Reiter is a masterful short story writer. Truth and humor are woven intricately, ripe with emotion and stripped down to the bone. You will read these again and again.

—Jacqueline Sheehan

New York Times bestselling author of *Lost and Found* (William Morrow) and *The Tiger in the House* (Kensington)

SUNSHOT PRESS

SUNSHOT PRESS WOULD NOT HAVE BEEN POSSIBLE WITHOUT
THE BOLD SUPPORT OF THE FOLLOWING POETS & WRITERS:

Barbara A.   Adrianne A.   T. A.   David A.   Idris A.   Kaye A.   Thomas J.   Paul M
Samantha T.   Linda F.   Craig O.   Gary P.   LeeAnn P.   Brian P.   Gary P.   T. M.
Ron V.   Marina H.   Eric W.   Sandra W.   Stuart W.   Emma W.   Fred W.
Rebecca L.   Barbara D.   Dana C.   Elaine C.   Kristen C.   Patricia B.
Timothy W.   James W.   Cynthia W.   Fred W.   Jeanne W.   Lee V.
Benjamin B.   Claire B.   Jerome   Marge B.   Patricia B.   Ruth M.
Barbara S.   Rachel B.   Ellen A.   Patricia R.   Nancy R.   Vincent J.
Alfred M.   Gregory S.   Jan S.   Catherine S.   James S.   Harvey S.
Lisa P.   Luke W.   Leland J.   Gail W.   Lillo W.   Pam W.   Lyzette W.
Terri M.   Sean M.   Deana N.   Jed M.   Barbra N.   Joel N.   Paul N.
Mara S. Ramon B.   Bruce R.   John R.   Jendi R.   Paddy R.   Susan P.
Stanley R.   Andrew S.   Lynn S.   Kathryn P.   Anneliese S.   Mick S.
Lones S.   Corey M.   Richard S.   Nathan S.   Andrew S.   Elaine S.
J.D. B.   Roberta D.   Susan S.   Victoria S.   Joanne S.   Jen S.
Felix N.   Evelyn V.   Derek U.   Mike T.   Naomi M.   Jayshiro T.
Simone M.   Aida Z.   Cindy Z.   Paula Z.   Allan Y.   Felice W.
Tori M.   Karen H.   Ken M.   Barbara M.   Matt M.   Sean M.
Anca H.   David H.   Dennis H.   Eileen H.   Linda H.   W. H.
Kate H.   Jack H.   Roberta H.   Eunice H.   Nancy H.
Jonathan G.   Bruce G.   Joshua B.   Thomas B.   Catherine B.   Enid H.
Susan C.   Danny C.   Laurie C.   Julius C.   Richard B.   R.C. G.   Adam G.
Casey C.   Garry C.   LaRue C.   Bob R.   Kathy C.   Susan C.   Margo B.
Rusty D.   Effie D.   Deborah D.   Annie D.   Howard G.
Bill G.   Tina G.   Nina G.   Paula F.   Jon F.
Jerri B.   Kathryn C.   Robynn C.   Greer G.
William E.   Mary D.   Frank D.   George D.
Ruth F.   Benjamin F.   Teressa E.   Renato E.
Chad F.   Andrew H.   Ann H.   Lorien H.   Jeff J.   Martin I.   Mark H.
Christina F.   Ellen L.   John L.   David L.   Djelloul M.   Bernard M.
Richard L.   Jeffrey M.   Kevin M.   Peter M.   Wendell M.   Clif M.
Genese G.   Howard E.   Alison L.   Kurt L.   Naomi L.   Sam L.
Albert L.   Patricia B.   Chad B.   Mark B.   David B.   Julia L.
Roberta G.   Olaf K.   Kristie L.   Jacqueline L.   Lee L.   Thom K.
Joanne G.   Francis J.   Joyce K.   Marylou S.   Peter K.
James C.   Jason H.   Ryan H.   Georganne H.   Cleda H.
Joan C.   Edie C.
Leslee B.
Beth C.
Jackie M.

THANK YOU

SUNSHOTS.ORG

SUNSHOT ⬡ PRESS